AN INTRODUCTION TO CONSULTEE-CENTERED CONSULTATION IN THE SCHOOLS

Drawing on historical writings about mental health consultation and on contemporary research and theory, Jonathan H. Sandoval lucidly explains the consultee-centered approach to consultation. The book provides an expert foundation on which to build a training program for future school-based consultants. Written for graduate students in school psychology, counselling psychology, special education, and social work, this book is an invaluable resource for mental health professionals working in schools who wish to upgrade their professional skills and grow as reflective practitioners. Individual chapters describe different stages in the consultation process, outline the processes characterized in each stage, detail useful consultant skills, review pertinent research, discuss the ethical principles underlying practice, and suggest self-monitoring questions for student consultants.

Featuring a step-by-step developmental model of the consultee-centered consultation process, this book encourages consultants to attend to those characteristics of the consultee that contribute to the work difficulty as well as evaluating the characteristics of the client and school setting that may play a role in the educator's problem. By detailing this unique approach, this concise volume provides an applicable, contextualized, and strategic form of consultation, and fosters a professional-to-professional relationship distinguishable from supervision, counseling, therapy, coaching, or other methods.

Jonathan H. Sandoval is Professor Emeritus at the University of California, Davis, USA.

Consultation and Intervention in School Psychology Series

Edited by Sylvia Rosenfield

Handbook of Research in School Consultation
William P. Erchul and Susan M. Sheridan

Handbook of Multicultural School Psychology: An Interdisciplinary Perspective
Emilia C. Lopez, Sara G. Nahari, Giselle B. Esquivel, Sherrie L. Proctor

Consultee-Centered Consultation: Improving the Quality of Professional Services in Schools and Community Organizations
Nadine M. Lambert, Ingrid Hylander, Jonathan Sandoval

Becoming a School Consultant: Lessons Learned
Sylvia Rosenfield

Crisis Counseling, Intervention and Prevention in the Schools, Third Edition
Jonathan H. Sandoval

An Introduction to Consultee-Centered Consultation in the Schools
Jonathan H. Sandoval

AN INTRODUCTION TO CONSULTEE-CENTERED CONSULTATION IN THE SCHOOLS

A Step-by-Step Guide to the Process and Skills

Jonathan H. Sandoval

Routledge
Taylor & Francis Group

NEW YORK AND LONDON

First published 2014
by Routledge
711 Third Avenue, New York, NY 10017

and by Routledge
2 Park Square, Milton Park, Abingdon, Oxon OX14 4RN

Routledge is an imprint of the Taylor & Francis Group, an informa business

© 2014 Taylor & Francis

The right of Jonathan H. Sandoval to be identified as author of this work has been asserted by him in accordance with sections 77 and 78 of the Copyright, Designs and Patents Act 1988.

Library of Congress Cataloging-in-Publication Data

Sandoval, Jonathan.
An introduction to consultee-centered consultation in the schools : a
    step-by-step guide to the process and skills / Jonathan H. Sandoval.
        pages cm. —(Consultation and intervention series in school psychology)
    Includes bibliographical references and index.
    1. School psychology.   2. Educational counseling.   3. Crisis
intervention (Mental health services)—United States.   4. Mental
health counselling—United States.   5. School children—Mental health
services.   I. Title.
    LB1027.55.S26 2013
    370.15—dc23
    2013026207

ISBN: 978-0-415-80773-9 (hbk)
ISBN: 978-0-415-80774-6 (pbk)
ISBN: 978-0-203-14581-4 (ebk)

Typeset in Bembo
by Apex CoVantage, LLC

For Susan Beecher Sandoval

CONTENTS

PREFACE

The impetus for this book came from conversations at the Fifth International Seminar on Consultee-Centered Consultation held in August 2008 in Boston. The topic of the conference was training and research on consultee-centered consultation. Among other topics, those present spent considerable time discussing what consultee-centered consultants need to learn and to be able to do. The group identified the need for an introductory exposition of the current theory and skills used in this approach to school-based consultation. This volume is one response to this challenge.

As I write this, it has been 20 years since the publication of *Mental Health Consultation and Collaboration* by Gerald Caplan and Ruth B. Caplan. That volume, and its predecessor from 1970, *The Theory and Practice of Mental Health Consultation*, have been the authoritative sources on mental health consultation and consultee-centered consultation for decades. However, since 1993 there have been changes and modifications to many of the ideas intrinsic to consultee-centered consultation, as it is practiced in school contexts internationally. We documented some of these changes in a book Nadine Lambert, Ingrid Hylander, and I coedited in 2004, *Consultee-Centered Consultation: Improving the Quality of Professional Services in Schools and Community Organizations.* That collection put forth many new ideas about consultee-centered consultation from veteran professionals working in Europe, Israel, and North America. The experiences of these practitioners and researchers and others in the past 10 years have continued to contribute to an expanded view of this important variety of school-based consultation. In the present volume I have organized and integrated the classic writings on consultee-centered mental health consultation with current findings and practices, with the intent to describe both the process of consultation and the techniques and skills involved. Many of these skills and practices are similar to those following other traditions of consultation, but that should come as no surprise.

I have been practicing, teaching, supervising, thinking, and writing about consultee-centered consultation for nearly 40 years. The reader will find me drawing on sources across the entire history of writings on mental health consultation. The early pioneers had much to teach us and we should not forget their contributions. Additionally, contemporary qualitative researchers have revealed a great deal new about what occurs between a consultant and a teacher struggling in their work with a child. I have not included case history illustrations in this presentation. Most of the sources in the references, particularly the older ones, include marvelous case examples of their practices and techniques. I encourage the reader to seek some of these out for further clarification of the consultation process.

There is no question that more research and study is needed on this model of school-based consultation. By making the consultee-centered model more explicit, I hope to inspire future scholars and practitioners to continue to refine what works in helping school professionals respond more effectively to the needs of their clients.

Contemporary consultee-centered consultants base their work on a number of theoretical approaches, including ideas from cognitive psychology, developmental psychology, and social psychology, and are aware of cultural and environmental factors that must be considered in the consultation the process. Caplan's basic concept of the prevention through working with adults who serve children still inspires us.

The first two chapters review the past and contemporary theoretical underpinnings of consultee-centered consultation as a type of mental health consultation. The next eight chapters present different phases of the process of consultation along with the skills consultants need to be successful. They offer a roadmap of how to proceed in a step-by-step fashion. Consultation is not always one-to-one, and I have included a chapter on consultee-centered consultation with groups of consultees. I conclude this introduction to consultation with a discussion of the ethical principles underlying practice. I hope the novice and experienced school-based consultant will benefit from a careful look at their practice and grow as reflective practitioners.

ACKNOWLEDGMENTS

First I must acknowledge the contribution of the late Nadine M. Lambert to my development as a school-based consultant. She introduced me to the promise of mental health consultation as a lens for viewing the work of psychologists in the schools, and to the inspirational writings of Gerald Caplan, Irving N. Berlin, and others during my student years at U.C. Berkeley. She was an early promoter of school-based consultation as part of the indirect service role of school psychologists. She was a wonderful teacher and colleague, and a good friend. She was indefatigable in her promotion of consultee-centered consultation. I must also mention the important role my consultation mentor and supervisor, Wilson Yandell, M.D., played in my thinking and understanding of the consultation process.

Over the years a number of colleagues from around the world have engaged in discussion and inspired me to rethink and reframe my conceptions about consultation. Ingrid Hylander, Gunilla Guvå, Colette Ingraham, Steven Knotek, Sylvia Rosenfield, and all the other participants in the five (so far) International Symposia on Consultee-Centered Consultation, have formed a supportive and brilliant community of like-minded scholars. It has been a pleasure to learn from you all. I hope I have done justice to their ideas in this book.

Finally I must acknowledge the contributions that John M. Davis had on my thinking. Jack and I cowrote several articles on mental health consultation and had many fruitful conversations at U.C. Davis when we worked together preparing school-based consultants. Many of the ideas in this book came from our joint efforts at puzzling through issues. Thank you all.

1

INTRODUCTION

Consultee-Centered Consultation and Prevention

No one profession or psychological specialty has an exclusive claim to the term *consultation*, nor is there any commonly agreed upon definition of the term. There are, however, some common elements to most conceptions. Nearly all authorities would acknowledge that it involves a helping relationship between a consultant and consultee, and that the consultant has some special knowledge or expertise that is needed by the consultee. Beyond this agreement, important differences stand out in the use of the term by different professionals and by adherents to different models of consultation within a profession.

Consultation in the Helping Professions

In business and in other nonhuman services fields, one turns to a consultant when something needs to be done that is outside of the range of expertise of the individuals on staff. Consultation means getting advice, training, or direct assistance in solving a problem. The consultant may assist the person seeking help, or may take over the job him or herself and complete it, moving on after the job is done. Thus, a company having problems with a manufacturing process will hire a consultant with appropriate expertise to solve the problem.

Usually two individuals are involved, a consultant and a consultee who may also be called a client (the client of the consultant). This form of consultation may be termed "expert consultation," and is hard to differentiate from instruction when the process is closely examined. The consultant tells the client/consultee what to do or does it for him or her.

Differences with the Helping Professions

In the helping professions, however, consultation is often thought about differently. Most experts identify three parties to consultation: the consultant (typically a mental health professional), the consultee (a staff member from another discipline), and the client (a patient). In this usage, the client is a client of the consultee, not the consultant. The problem the consultant helps with involves the relationship between the consultee and the client in the work setting. Thus, the consultant assists the consultee to become more effective with the consultee's clients.

In education, for example, consultation is thought of as a process of interaction between two professional persons, a consultant, who is a special services provider and an expert in some area of psychology or mental health, and the consultee, who is a teacher or administrator who is an expert in curriculum or pedagogy. The topic of consultation is the consultee's client(s), or work related problems most often involving children, groups of children, or their parents. Contributions to the solution of the work problem come from the joint problem solving effort of the consultant and consultee. The educator's work problem involves the management or education of one or more students in a classroom or, in the case of school administrator consultees, school personnel or school policies. The consultant and consultee share accountability for the planning and implementation of a program to cater to student needs. Consultation may involve more than one consultant and more than one consultee at a time (Heron & Harris, 1987; Idol, Paolucci-Whitcomb, & Nevin, 1995). In the literature in counseling, school psychology, and school social work, consultation has been defined as a service delivery model, as a professional role, as an intervention, or as a delivery system for creating interventions (Frank & Kratochwill, 2008; Meyers, Parsons, & Martin, 1979). There is some basis for all of these characterizations.

Certain features of human services consultation are different from practices in nonhelping professions. Besides the differentiation of the client and consultee, distinguishing features include the ideas of *mutual problem solving* and *mutual responsibility*. Mutual problem solving is common to most conceptualizations of consultation in the educational arena. Since each participant brings different skills and knowledge to the table, by blending them through conversation, new ideas can emerge. There will be a higher probability that the target problem may be successfully addressed than if each participant had worked on the problem alone. The basic notion is that two or more heads (and two or more theories) are better than one. Mutual problem solving also implies that the relationship is nonhierarchical, and that a positive, collaborative working relationship has been established.

Mutual responsibility is present in that both the consultant and consultee have some responsibility to the client and to the system in which they work. The consultee has direct responsibility for the client; that is, the teacher is chiefly accountable for the learning and development of his or her pupils. The consultant has an ethical responsibility for the welfare of the client, and a professional responsibility to the system, but little direct control over what happens in the classroom.

In addition, human services consultation "enables" or "empowers" consultees. As the process generates new understandings and the consultee practices new skills, the consultee grows as a professional. Professional self-esteem comes from solving difficult human problems, and self-confidence increases the motivation to take on new challenges.

Another feature of human services consultation is that it is an *indirect* service to children. It is an effort by school psychologists, counselors, and social workers to enhance, by collaborative problem solving, the understandings and skills of the adults who work directly with the children. Children benefit most from changes in the behavior of adults, such as teachers and parents, with whom they spend the majority of their time. Paradoxically, mental health workers in the schools often have the greatest impact when they work indirectly on children's behalf (Gutkin & Conoley, 1990; Sheridan & Gutkin, 2000). Although consultation is only one part of the role of the school mental health worker, it is an important one. Other direct roles may include assessment, teaching, counseling, and working with parents, but typically these activities impact only a small group or one client at a time.

In addition, human services consultation is usually thought of as experimental. No attempts to solve human problems are foolproof, and all attempts to solve problems must be viewed as experimental undertakings. That is, possible interventions must be treated as hypotheses to be tested and verified. Consultation should involve data collection and evaluation. Formative evaluation leads to more responsive intervention.

Ideally consultation is educational for the participants. Both the consultee and the consultant will learn from each other as a result of the consultation conversation. Since each is bringing expertise from a different field (psychology versus pedagogy, for example), they will be exposed to new ideas and points of view.

Once a problem is defined in consultation, if the process is done carefully and clearly, interventions will emerge. As will be discussed in a later chapter, sometimes the working relationship between the consultee and client will improve following consultation with no explicit intervention devised. But usually the goal of consultation is to plan changes to the work setting that will enable the client to be successful.

The consultation or collaboration process, then, is a companion to other services provided by special services personnel. School psychologists, resource specialists, speech and language therapists, counselors, social workers, and others will continue to deliver traditional services. The goal of the problem solving that occurs between the consultant and the consultee is to enhance or support the consultee's skills rather than to "tell" them what to do. The fundamental intentions of consultation are to improve outcomes for the consultee's current clients and to increase the consultee's ability to work with future, similar clients.

What Consultation Is Not

Consultation is not *supervision,* because collaborative consultation cannot function freely if the consultant is also viewed as supervisor or evaluator. Nor is it

TABLE 1.1 The parameters of consultation

Consultation Is	Consultation Is Not
*Enabling	*Supervising
*An indirect service to the client	*A direct service to the client
*Mutual problem solving	*Counseling or psychotherapy
*Experimental	*Advice or reassurance giving
*Educational for the participants	*Teaching or supervising the consultee
*To generate interventions	*To label a child

teaching, because there is no set agenda for what is covered in the consultation relationship. The process of consultation is educational for all concerned but it is not a teacher-learner relationship. Although they share some techniques in common, consultation is not *counseling* or *psychotherapy,* because the focus is clearly on work related problems, not intrapsychic conflicts. The educators' and consultant's private lives and interpersonal relations outside of the school are not the focus of the problem solving.

Finally, consultation is not a *substitute for other roles* held by the consultant, because the school-based professional will still need to fill other roles and provide other services. Pupil personnel workers will continue to test, counsel, teach, and deliver other direct services to children. Table 1.1 summarizes the parameters of consultation.

What the Consultant Contributes

If the consultee brings work problems to consultation, what does the consultant bring? In addition to contributing a particular set of knowledge from his or her discipline, as outlined previously, consultants also take responsibility for the consultation process once a consultee requests help. They are responsible for taking leadership in asking questions about the problem situation, for seeing to it that the problem is defined in a clear way, for reviewing past efforts to address the problem, for helping develop a set of interventions coming from the consultee's thoughts about what is a workable solution, and for generating suggestions from psychological knowledge and theory. They often assist in collecting objective information in order to produce more ideas about the child so that the problem may be better defined (Sandoval, Lambert, & Davis, 1977). This data collection may be done by observation, informal assessment, formal assessment, or interview. The consultant is also responsible for evaluating how effective a particular intervention has been, for documenting what has occurred in collaboration, and for recording successful and unsuccessful interventions. Thus, in addition to information from their field, the consultant must also be knowledgeable about the techniques and the process of consultation.

Just how the process occurs and what expert knowledge is used in educational consultation varies from consultation approach to approach. The various schools of educational consultation have more in common than not, yet most authorities differentiate among types of consultation. Traditionally in the school psychology literature, for example, there has been a distinction between behavioral, organizational, and mental health consultation. Recent variants of these three types, such as conjoint behavioral consultation, instructional consultation, and consultee-centered consultation, have emerged and been researched (Erchul & Sheridan, 2008). This book will detail the single model of consultation practice called consultee-centered consultation, which has evolved from the older model, mental health consultation.

Mental Health Consultation

Mental health consultation is one of the oldest approaches to consultation developed by psychological professionals. It grew out of the preventive psychiatry movement starting in the 1940s. Early pioneers include Coleman (1947), Maddux (1950, 1955), Bindman (1959), Caplan (1964, 1970), Parker (1958), and Berlin (1956). Most of the founders were psychiatrists and psychoanalysts who consulted with public agencies, including schools. The most influential of these first leaders was Gerald Caplan, whose 1970 book *The Theory and Practice of Mental Health Consultation* defined the field. Caplan identified four types of consultation: (1) client-centered case consultation, (2) consultee-centered case consultation, (3) program-centered administrative consultation, and (4) consultee-centered administrative consultation. Both case consultation, which involves attention to problems with clients or groups of clients, and administrative consultation, which involves attention to problems with systems and programs, were further divided into those that center on either the client or the consultee. The variety with which this book is concerned is the latter.

Consultation that is focused on the consultee prioritizes the characteristics of the consultee that are contributing to his or her work difficulty, while involving little or no direct assessment of the client. The goal is to assist the consultee to overcome impediments to working productively with a client. Caplan considered there to be four major sources of work difficulty: (1) lack of knowledge, (2) lack of skill, (3) lack of confidence, and (4) lack of objectivity. He developed consultant strategies and responses to address each of these impediments. Important premises of this type of consultation are that the consultee initiates the contact, making it a voluntary relationship; the consultant has no administrative responsibility with respect to the consultee; the consultation is time limited; and the consultee is free to accept or reject any ideas about how to behave differently with the client. In addition the process fosters professional development in consultees, and makes them better able to address the needs of future clients. Thus consultation assumes a professional-to-professional relationship, and is distinguished from supervision, counseling, therapy, education, and collaboration.

In contrast, client-centered consultation puts the emphasis on solving the particular issue with the client. The process is hierarchical, in that the consultant takes a much more active role in assessing the client and designing interventions to address the problem. It is prescriptive, in that the consultant brings a particular expertise and theoretical orientation to the process. In school-based practice, an example of client-centered consultation might be behavioral consultation.

Caplan's consultee-centered consultation has come to be the "classic" model of mental health consultation and as such, will be referred to and expanded upon throughout this volume. He is one the major theorists in the area and his book has done much to foster its growth and development around the world. However, Caplan based his notions about consultation on his experiences as a consultant coming from the outside of the system where he consulted. The same is true of other early pioneers such as Irving N. Berlin.

School-based consultants have been less familiar with the work of Berlin (1964, 1969, 1977). Although he did not build as formidable a system as Caplan, a similar consultee-centered approach emerged from his writings. His descriptions of the process of consultation were succinct and profound. Berlin stated,

> The method involves a diagnostic appraisal of the conflicts which cause the work problem; dynamic understanding of the anxieties and of the form in which they are presented to the consultant; efforts to reduce the anxieties by the consultant's comments (which indicate his understanding); acceptance and personal experience with similar feelings; and conflicts engendered in the consultee by the behavior of his clients; and finally, discussion of how similar problems have been or may be handled by others so that the consultee can get some sense of how he might deal with the problem he presents. (Berlin, 1964, p. 259)

Issues with Mental Health Consultation

The descriptor *mental health* in mental health consultation and the psychiatric background of its pioneers has led to some misconceptions about this model of consultation. First, because Caplan was psychoanalytically trained, many assume that Freudian theory is the main underpinning for this process. Although psychodynamic theory has great value in the consultation process, other psychological theories also have an important place in understanding the work problems of a consultee. Current conceptions of consultee-centered consultation emphasize the use of a multitude of behavioral, cognitive, and developmental theories to understand consultees and clients, as the reader will learn in the following chapters.

Second, the idea of mental health in the label implies that the consultee is not mentally healthy and that the consultee is receiving a psychological treatment. In fact, Caplan's intent was to communicate that the ultimate outcome of consultation was mental health promotion—to improve mental health and educational outcomes for future clients of the consultee, not the consultee him or herself. Caplan's public health background led to his hope to make primary institutions like the school more effective in promoting healthy mental and physical development through assisting key personnel.

Alternatively, the label mental health may also imply that mental health problems in clients are the only subject to be discussed. Consultees may bring to consultation any work-related problem, and in schools these problems may involve instructional issues.

In spite of these misconceptions and the difference between coming to the schools as an outside consultant (e.g., Caplan, Berlin) and being employed by the consultee's institution (e.g., most school psychologists, counselors, and social workers), consultants in the United States, Scandinavia, Europe, and Israel have continued to develop the practice and theory of consultee-centered consultation (Lambert, Hylander, & Sandoval, 2004). To avoid some of the past misconceptions and to capture some new ideas from contemporary practice, many school psychologists following this model have chosen to use the label *consultee-centered consultation* rather than the more generic label *mental health consultation*.

Collaboration

The term collaboration is another one that is in widespread use and is even used to modify consultation, as in *collaborative* consultation. In his revision of his 1970 book (Caplan & Caplan, 1993) Caplan added the concept of collaboration to the title and the discussion. The distinction he drew between collaboration and consultation is that in the former, the consultant accepts responsibility for the outcome of the client and functions as a part of the professional team diagnosing and treating the client. In addition, the mental health collaborator is a member, a coequal, of the institutional staff, not an outsider. Although individual collaborators have a coordinate status with other professionals, they have hierarchical authority for decisions within their professional domains, such as providing counseling. Also, in collaboration there is a mutual educative function where each member of the staff potentially increases their understanding and skill as a result of exposure to other ways of thinking. The concept of collaboration fits much of what mental health professionals do in schools. They serve on individual educational programming teams and on other multidisciplinary teams in schools. But the focus in this book will be on consultation, the more informal meetings between pupil personnel workers and others in the school setting. The indirect service provided by consultants outside of the team process has its own value, acknowledging the fact that there is huge overlap between the concept of consultation and collaboration activities.

Consultee-Centered Consultation

Over the years, as those with training and interest in mental health consultation have adapted it for practice in the schools, there has been a continuing discussion about how Caplan's ideas can be translated in to practice. Caplan's book has enjoyed international popularity with consultants throughout the world. Those working in educational settings, particularly, have been guided by his conceptions, although they have added their own ideas to the model, based on their research and practice in the schools. To date, five international conferences have been held to discuss continuing developments in consultee-centered consultation since the publication of Caplan's book. Participants including Caplan developed the following definition in 1999:

> Consultee-centered consultation emphasizes a nonhierarchical, nonprescriptive helping role relationship between a resource (consultant) and a person or group (consultee) who seeks professional help with a work problem involving a third party (client).
>
> This work problem is a topic of concern for the consultee who has a direct responsibility for the learning, development or productivity of the client.
>
> The primary task of both the consultant and consultee is to choose and reframe knowledge about wellbeing, development, intrapersonal, interpersonal and organizational effectiveness appropriate to the consultee's work setting.
>
> The goal of the consultation process is the joint development of a new way of conceptualizing the work problem so that the repertoire of the consultee is expanded and the professional relationship between the consultee and the client is restored or improved. (Lambert, 2004, pp. 11–12)

Subsequent chapters illuminate this definition. The next chapter will cover contemporary conceptions of consultee-centered consultation in more detail, drawing on cognitive and developmental psychology, and will provide a road map of the process. Later chapters will discuss the techniques used to achieve consultee-centered goals, and the issues raised in the practice of consultee-centered consultation.

Consultee-Centered Consultation and Prevention

For many years, psychologists and other social scientists have researched topics that are closely related to education. Increasingly the work of educational psychologists has become the source of new methods and techniques in teaching and organizing subject matter. Whereas previously philosophers and subject matter specialists such as mathematicians or literature critics had the most important voice in dictating curriculum, now educators include psychological principles in planning their practice.

The field of education clearly has psychological foundations. Most teachers are formally exposed to educational psychology during their teacher education programs, and some may have majored in psychology or human development as undergraduates. Unfortunately theories and principles of psychology are seldom learned in the context of day-to-day classroom life and applied to particular individual children. As a result, psychological consultation provides an opportunity for educators to revisit and personalize many ideas they have had exposure to but have not integrated into their practice. It is also the case that a number of psychological theories and topics are absent from courses on educational psychology, and the consultant will bring a number of new ideas from the discipline to the consultation conversation.

Consultee-centered consultation evolved from and aims to be a part of efforts to promote healthy cognitive, emotional, and social development and to prevent educational failure. Prevention, as an activity, has the goal of reducing the possibility that an undesired event or condition occurs. Should the condition in fact occur, prevention also aims at reducing the severity of negative consequences. Three levels of prevention are usually identified: primary, secondary, and tertiary. Other labels are "school-wide" or "universal," "targeted," and "intensive."

Primary prevention occurs when preventive activities are directed at the entire population. Primary prevention interventions are provided to everyone in the hope that no one will develop the condition. Usually primary prevention takes place in primary institutions; that is, in institutions that serve the total population. An example from public health is the construction of clean water systems and modern sewer systems for an entire village to prevent diphtheria and typhus. Everyone in the village is protected by a basic intervention. Compulsory education for all in fully developed countries may be considered an effort at the primary prevention of the exploitation of the people by demagogues. Making education as effective as possible can prevent superstition, ignorance, unemployment, and worker nonproductivity.

Secondary prevention refers to efforts or interventions directed only at populations who are at risk of developing a condition. People who live near still bodies of water in tropical areas, for example, are more at risk of contracting malaria than those who live in the mosquito-free mountains. Programs of mosquito abatement or the use of quinine for the jungle dwellers is an example of secondary prevention. Preschool programs for children living in poverty to promote early academic success would be an example of secondary educational prevention.

Tertiary prevention takes place when interventions are made to keep an already existing problem from getting worse. To continue with a medical example, the use of antibiotics for an infection is preventative in that it keeps the infection from getting worse and/or fatal. Tertiary prevention in an educational setting might be to work with pupils who have failed a preliminary examination in the hope that this extra tutoring will prevent a failure on the final examination.

Tertiary prevention is perhaps the most common level of prevention now performed in the schools. School psychologists and other pupil services personnel most often work with pupils who have already developed problems manifested in the classroom. The hope is to prevent these problems from becoming worse. Special education programs such as classes for the developmentally delayed or emotionally disturbed are attempts to educate children in spite of existing conditions, which, if untreated, would result in children dropping out of school as illiterates.

Tertiary programs such as these are valuable and necessary, but are relatively expensive and time-consuming when compared to some primary and secondary prevention programs. Just as it is easier to give a preventative injection than to treat typhoid, it is often less expensive and more humane to set up educational programs that have the objective of preventing future failure, than to address long-term outcomes of unemployment and crime.

In spite of cost and other advantages, primary and secondary preventions are not often done in educational settings. One reason is best expressed by the saying "when you are surrounded by alligators, it is difficult to remember to drain the swamp." Because there are so many children and teachers in educational institutions who are in crisis or who have serious problems, they get priority. School psychologists and educational psychologists must attend to emergency needs and work at tertiary prevention. There is no time left to do primary and secondary prevention—to drain the swamp.

A second reason why primary and secondary prevention is ignored is the problem of evaluation. If one is effective in doing primary and secondary prevention, the result is that no problems occur. When fewer or no problems occur, people have nothing concrete to remind them of the need for the service. Without an easily observable need, the cost of prevention seems excessive. In medicine, immunologists have been very successful at developing a number of vaccines for childhood illnesses. At present, the fear of such killers as polio, German measles, whooping cough, and diphtheria has decreased as a result of such successes, and parents have begun to become complacent. The outcome of the success has been that immunizations have been skipped and many of these diseases have been making a comeback. As a result, it is still necessary to be able to defend and justify one's efforts at primary and secondary prevention so that others will not believe prevention efforts are foolish and wasteful.

A different difficulty in evaluation is the fact that few preventative programs in education, including consultation, have been thoroughly documented as being effective (Zins, 2007). When not 100% effective, or when positive evidence is accompanied by negative findings, it is usually easy to remember the failures. Prevention often suffers when budgets are tight.

In spite of the problem of finding the time to do primary and secondary prevention, and the problem of evaluating and justifying one's efforts, the advantages of prevention should be clear. In the long run prevention is more efficient and economical. Educational failure is very costly to society. Educational failure means that individuals will not be able to assume their rightful place in society and society will not function effectively as a result.

Consultee-centered consultation is often thought of as a primary prevention technique. However, the process, when well executed, is both a primary and secondary intervention. The outcome of consultation is usually a variety of strategies or interventions the consultee may use to help the client. In this sense the client may be considered "at-risk," and consultation would then be a secondary prevention. However, the consultation could also be educational and add to the consultee's repertoire of interventions for use with future clients, thus being primary as well as secondary. Or, another way it could be preventive is when the consultation has helped the consultee come to an awareness of how he or she might deliver preventive services to clients in general (Zins, 2007). Consultee-centered consultation should have secondary prevention as its immediate focus but with primary prevention as its major goal.

The provision of consultant services is an important way for psychologists and others to act preventively. By consulting with teachers about children or with administrators about parents, teachers, and children, the consultant helps the consultee improve his or her professional functioning, and as a result, the consultee may become more effective with a given child or teacher as well as future children or teachers. Children can be helped not to fail by expanding the repertoire of the educator's behavior.

One goal of the Regular Education Initiative (Will, 1986) in special education was to enable teachers in regular classrooms to work more effectively with children at risk or who have been identified as having educational disabilities. This movement however, has created additional stresses on teachers who are required to cope with a large range of individual differences. Resistance to inclusion has come about as a result of fear and anxiety of the unknowns in teaching students with disabilities alongside general education students. There has been a need to increase resources to the regular education teacher in the form of consultation.

Consultation is an important activity for professionals interested in prevention. This book will explicate the process of consultation following a model based on consultee-centered consultation, but modified in important ways to fit the special role of the school-based consultant.

References

Altrocchi, J. (1972). Mental health consultation. In S.E. Golann and C. Eisdorfer (Eds.), *Handbook of community mental health* (pp. 477–508). New York: Appleton-Century-Crofts.

Berlin, I.N. (1956). Some learning experiences as psychiatric consultant in schools. *Mental Hygiene, 40,* 215–236.

Berlin, I.N. (1964). Learning mental health consultation history and problems. *Mental Hygiene, 48,* 257–266.

Berlin, I.N. (1969). Mental health consultation for school social workers: A conceptual model. *Community Mental Health Journal, 5,* 280–288.

Berlin, I. (1977). Some lessons learned in 25 years of mental health consultation to schools. In S.C. Plog & P.I. Ahmed (Eds.), *Principles and techniques of mental health consultation* (pp. 23–48). New York: Plenum Publishing Corporation.

Bindman, A.J. (1959). Mental health consultation: Theory and practice. *Journal of Consulting Psychology, 23*, 473–482.

Caplan, G. (1964). *Principles of preventative psychiatry.* New York: Basic Books.

Caplan, G. (1970). *The theory and practice of mental health consultation.* New York: Basic Books.

Caplan, G., & Caplan, R.B. (1993). *Mental health consultation and collaboration.* San Francisco: Jossey-Bass.

Coleman, J.R. (1947). Psychiatric consultation in casework agencies. *American Journal of Orthopsychiatry, 17*, 533–539.

Erchul, W.P., & Sheridan S.M. (2008). *Handbook of research in school consultation.* New York: Erlbaum/Taylor & Francis.

Frank, J.L., & Kratochwill, T.R. (2008). School-based problem-solving consultation. In W.P. Erchul & S.M. Sheridan (Eds.), *Handbook of research in school consultation* (pp. 13–30). New York: Erlbaum/Taylor & Francis.

Gutkin, T.B., & Conoley, J.C. (1990). Reconceptualizing school psychology from a service delivery perspective: Implications of practice, training, and research. *Journal of School Psychology, 28*, 202–223.

Heron, T.E., & Harris, K.C. (1987). *The educational consultant: Helping professionals, parents and mainstreamed students* (2nd ed.). Austin, TX: Pro-ed Publishers.

Idol, L., Paolucci-Whitcomb, P., & Nevin, A. (1995). The collaborative consultation model. *Journal of Educational and Psychological Consultation, 6*, 329–346.

Lambert, N.M. (2004). Consultee-centered consultation; an international perspective in goals, process, and theory. In N. M Lambert, I. Hylander, & J. H Sandoval (Eds.), *Consultee-centered consultation* (pp. 3–19). Mahwah, NJ: Lawrence Erlbaum.

Lambert, N.M., Hylander, I., & Sandoval, J. (Eds.). (2004). *Consultee-centered consultation: Improving the quality of professional services in schools and community organizations.* Mahwah, NJ: Lawrence Erlbaum.

Maddux, J.F. (1950). Psychiatric consultation in a public welfare agency. *American Journal of Orthopsychiatry, 20*, 754–764.

Maddux, J.F. (1955). Consultation in public health. *American Journal of Public Health, 45*, 1424–1430.

Meyers, J., Parsons, R.D., & Martin, R. (1979). *Mental health consultation in the schools.* San Francisco: Jossey-Bass Publishers.

Parker, B. (1958). *Psychiatric consultation for nonpsychiatric professional workers* (Public Health Monograph #53). Washington, DC: U.S. Department of Health, Education, and Welfare.

Sandoval, J., Lambert, N.M., & Davis, J.M. (1977). Consultation from the consultee's perspective. *Journal of School Psychology, 15*, 334–342.

Sheridan, S.M., & Gutkin, T.B. (2000). The ecology of school psychology: Examining and changing our paradigm for the 21st century. *School Psychology Review, 29*, 485–502.

Will, M. (1986). Educating children with learning problems: A shared responsibility. *Exceptional Children, 52*, 411–415.

Zins, J.E. (2007). Has consultation achieved its primary prevention potential? *Journal of Educational and Psychological Consultation, 17*, 133–150.

2

CONTEMPORARY CONSULTEE-CENTERED CONSULTATION THEORY

When a child is having difficulty in school, the explanation often focuses on deficits in the child. School mental health workers along with teachers analyze the child's behavior, collect test data, and offer a diagnosis and an intervention or treatment plan. Oftentimes the intervention does involve teachers changing the way they interact with the child, or the provision of additional resources, but the perception persists that it is in response to a lack in the child's background and make-up.

An alternative stance explains the difficulty as residing in the match between the child and the teacher or institution. The child may have deficits as well as strengths, but the teacher and the school, too, are deficient in accommodating to the child's individuality. A change must occur in the relationship between the teacher or school and the child to address the problem. The focus is simultaneously on the child and on the teacher and school.

This is a subtle distinction, one that is a matter of degree or emphasis. This second stance, however, is at the heart of consultee-centered mental health consultation. Consultee-centered consultation puts an emphasis on the characteristics of the consultee that are contributing to his or her work difficulty, and involves little or no direct assessment of the client by the consultant. Although some objective information about the client will be useful, the process highlights the consultee's subjective interpretation of the client's behavior. In addition the process explores how other aspects of the consultee's professional knowledge and skill may contribute to the professional dilemma. In the end, consultation should improve the professional functioning of the consultee, and restore the consultee's working relationship with the client.

To review, according to Caplan (1970), in consultee-centered consultation the outside consultant has no administrative responsibility for the consultee's work, and no professional responsibility for the outcome of the client's case. The consultant has no authority to modify the consultee's behavior toward the client. Because consultation is voluntary, the consultee has no need to accept the consultant's ideas or suggestions. There is a coequal or coordinate relationship between the consultant and consultee and an understanding that together they will discuss the work problem, sharing respective views of the problem from their own perspectives. The discussion about the client occurs between two professional equals. The consultant, being a member of another profession, will contribute information about psychological theory and mental health. Another feature is that the consultant has no predetermined body of information, specific theoretical stance, or agenda to impart to the consultee. The consultant acknowledges that the consultee has relevant expertise about the client's work problem and works to bring out this knowledge in the consultation process. The consultant hopes to help the consultee improve the handling or understanding of the current work problem with the goal of assisting the consultee to manage similar problems in the future. The aim is to improve the consultee's job performance and not necessarily his or her general sense of well-being. Consultee-centered consultation does not involve the discussion of personal or private material, and the consultation process is understood to be a privileged communication on the part of the consultant. The responsibility for the outcome of the client remains with the consultant.

School-based consultants follow this model but acknowledge that they do have indirect responsibility for the client. If consultation is not successful in resolving an issue with a child, a different form of involvement with the consultee may become necessary, such as joint membership on a multidisciplinary team. Although consultation is voluntary, there may be institutional pressures for consultees to request consultation.

Caplan's Sources of Consultee Difficulty

Caplan (1963) has identified four major categories of difficulty that bring a consultee to consultation: (a) lack of understanding of the psychological factors in the case; (b) lack of skill or resources to deal with the problems involved; (c) lack of confidence and self-esteem due to fatigue, illness, inexperience, youth, or old age; and (d) lack of professional objectivity in handling the case. Category (a) may indicate a missing conceptualization or a naive idea about the causes of the problem with a client. Category (b) relates to missing procedural knowledge about how to address a problem or the tools to implement a change in the classroom. Both of these sources imply the need for new learning. Categories (c) and (d) suggest that affect or emotion, either manifest or hidden, may be contributing to the work difficulty. These latter two sources of difficulty imply the need for help in emotional regulation and learning.

Consultee-Centered Consultation: Facilitating Learning and Managing Emotion

Consultee-centered consultation, then, has two important aspects: It involves learning new skills and knowledge and it involves managing emotion. Consultee-centered consultants use techniques and methods to address all four of Caplan's sources of difficulty. The process will result in new learning on the part of the consultant and on the part of the consultee. Some of the learning will be specific to the case, and some will be more general about professional roles.

In addition, the process must deal with emotion, since the consultation dilemma and process itself often evokes strong feelings within the consultee and within the consultant. The consultee, and sometimes the consultant, will enter consultation with a number of sentiments about the work problem, about the client, and about him or herself as professional. In asking for help, many consultees will be making an admission of failure and professional incompetence. Feelings of shame or embarrassment may be present and need to be ameliorated.

Consultants, on the other hand, will enter consultation with expectations that they can be helpful, yet will be facing problems of great complexity that may have frustrated the consultee and others for a long time. Often they will feel like they are being tested, which can bring anxiety and a sense of urgency. They may be sensitive to certain kinds of problems based on life experiences and a lack of objectivity themselves (Berlin, 1966).

Facilitating Learning: Conceptual Change in Consultation

Both consultees and consultants will learn something new as a result of consultation. They will learn something new about the client, the process of consultation, their profession, and themselves. The stance in consultee-centered consultation is that through consultation they will construct new understandings in all four domains, changing or elaborating old conceptions. One of the theoretical foundations of consultee-centered consultation is constructivism. Constructivism is both an epistemology, and an approach to learning and teaching. Constructivism (like "consultation") has a number of different definitions and meanings, but at the heart is the idea that each individual constructs their own, possibly unique, understanding of how the world works. Different ideas from constructivist theory, particularly conceptual change theory, have important implications for consultation practice.

Three Views of Constructivism

Henning-Stout has written about constructivism as a postmodern epistemology that she characterizes as a "feminine" way of knowing. Consultation and constructivism are related, in this view, when consultation consists of "constructing understanding collectively, suspending expert agendas in order to 'listen' to the situation and the people involved, and adapting to the requirements revealed with that listening"(Henning-Stout, 1994, p. 12). The relationship between the consultant and consultee in this approach is collaborative and connected. Consultee-centered consultation, with its emphasis on the interpersonal relationship between the consultant and the consultee, is consistent with this notion of constructivism.

Cobern (1993) described a second aspect of constructivism: a model of the learning process. The central tenant in this perspective is that the learner is always an active agent in the learning process, not a passive participant receiving transmitted information. Piaget, for one, advocated this view of the learner. Translated into instructional theory, the classroom must be organized so as to permit students to explore and discuss different explanations of phenomena and to build their own understandings. Translated into consultation theory, the consultee must be an active participant in the consultation process. In consultation both participants will be constructing new understandings through "play" with ideas and exploration of new information.

A third aspect of constructivism is the notion of the development and change of cognitive constructions, or schema, over time. As individuals grow older and gain more experience solving problems in the external world, they build or construct their own theories about how things work. These theories or conceptions of the physical and interpersonal world are influenced by what they observe, are told, or deduce from their interactions at home, in the neighborhood, in the community, and in formal educational settings. Developmentalists, such as Piaget, have documented qualitative changes in thinking over time in children and adults. Young children's explanations of phenomena are often quite different from adults' explanations. In addition, the theorist Vygotsky has illustrated how social interaction, such as between the consultant and consultee, is important for intellectual growth and change (Van der Veer & Valsiner, 1991).

Conceptual Change

It is clear that conceptual shifting continues, in most domains, throughout our lifetime as we are exposed to new information. Scholars of the history of science have noted that ideas about the physical world have changed over time as well. In science, as research and theory progress, there have been paradigm shifts that lead to important changes in how everyone understands the world (Kuhn, 1962). For a paradigm to change, scientists have to confront and address anomalies in the currently accepted paradigm. When enough significant anomalies have occurred to create a crisis, motivation exists to examine new ideas, even ones previously discarded, in an effort to build a new model. The new model may create a paradigm shift if it is better at explaining and predicting phenomena than the previous model.

As consultants, we also see and often hope to observe paradigm shifts in our consultees and in ourselves. We hope that as an outcome of consultation, our consultees come to understand their clients in a new way, one that enables them to be more helpful in their professional roles. In a sense, consultation can be an important tool for professional development, although consultees do not come with this outcome in mind.

Science teachers and researchers have found that for change and new learning to occur, four conditions identified by Posner, Strike, Hewson, and Gertzog (1982) must be present: (a) a dissatisfaction with existing conceptions, (b) a new conception that is intelligible, (c) a new conception that is initially plausible, and (d) a new conception that, if fruitful, suggests the possibility of solving additional problems. If these conditions are part of an instructional program, students will accommodate, in the Piagetian sense, and change conceptual schema rather than assimilate new information into their old ones.

Conceptual change in consultation

Consultee-centered consultation has processes similar to those used in the teaching of science. In consultation we assume that a consultee, upon entering consultation, often has a conception of why a client is behaving the way he or she does. However, acting on this conception, the consultee has not been successful in addressing the client's needs. This failure of the model is often what brings the consultee to consultation: The consultee's construction of the situation, if not naive, at least is not working to permit the consultee to be effective with the client. The task facing the consultant is to explore with the consultee new ways of theorizing about the problems and puzzles facing the consultee. The two will reexamine old information about the client and possibly collect new information to test new hypotheses. The hope is that a new conceptual schema will emerge, one that will lead to richer understandings and productive interventions with clients. The consultant must begin by determining the consultee's understanding of the client's situation and the consultee's theory about why the problem exists.

As the process proceeds, the consultant and consultee will likely explore how the consultee's construction is inadequate to explain this and other cases. Particularly by the presentation of anomalous data—pointing out where the theory does not work and by highlighting dissonant evidence not predicted by the consultee's framework—the consultant helps build dissatisfaction with the current explanatory theory. When a new theory is put forward during consultation, it must be an understandable substitute. It must be intelligible, coherent, and internally consistent and seem like a plausible explanation. Finally, the new idea must seem to have widespread applicability—it should be elegant, parsimonious, and efficacious in working with future clients and problems as well as the current client and problem. It should explain more of the observed facts of the case than the previous theory. As with science instruction, the focus will be on anomalies; that is, how existing notions about the problem fail to explain all the facts about the situation or produce interventions.

Eventually a new theory will be produced by the consultation. It may be proposed by the consultant or by the consultee (or consultees, if it is a group consultation). Often analogies and metaphors will be used to introduce the new ideas and conceptualizations and make them intelligible to both the consultant and consultee. Although analogies may be useful initially, it is important to be sure that the correct features are abstracted from the analogy and transferred to the new theory.

Unlike the teaching of science, where there is a goal to bring the learner to the point of thinking like a scientist, the goal in consultation is not necessarily to have the consultee adopt the theories of the consultant. Instead the intent is for there to be a mutual construction of conceptualization that fits the situation and permits action. This openness makes the new understanding that is the outcome of consultation unknown and unpredictable, but also makes the process more enjoyable and challenging.

Consultation Processes Related to New Learning and Conceptual Change

It is the *process* of interaction during consultee-centered consultation that leads to changes or shifts in the consultee's understanding and behavior toward the client. To examine process, qualitative research has provided evidence about what is effective in naturalistic settings with experienced consultee-centered consultants.

Modes of Interaction

Working in Sweden, Hylander (2000, 2012) created a grounded theory based on what skilled, effective consultants trained in Caplan's model actually do in practice. She illuminated how three modes of interaction characterize consultee-centered consultation at different times. The skilled use of these modes results in conceptual change in the consultant and the consultee. Hylander described the approach mode, the free neutral mode, and the moving away mode. The approach mode involves the consultant helping the consultee describe the dilemma (presentation), seeking to understand underlying thoughts about the causes of the problem (representations), and allowing the consultee to discharge feelings and express negative thoughts. In this mode, consultants demonstrate they can understand and appreciate the point of view of the consultee.

The free neutral mode involves the school psychologist and the consultee freely exchanging thoughts and ideas about the dilemma. The school psychologist provides structure and focus through asking questions and sharing different perspectives. In this mode, the consultant and the consultee generate hypotheses about what might be happening, and examine the situation in multiple ways.

The moving away mode gets its name from both the consultee and consultant moving away from the old ways of understanding the problem and toward new ways of intervening with the client, based on a shift in the consultee's (and consultant's) representation. The consultant challenges the old ideas by introducing new information, more satisfactory explanations for behavior, and perspectives from psychological theory. The consultee and the consultant are discovering a new way to frame the dilemma.

Hylander's (2012) theory is not a stage theory. She notes that the process of consultation involves shifting back and forth between the modes, but never directly between the approach mode and moving away mode without moving through the free neutral mode. In her grounded theory, she points out how the process may result in change and how it may fail, either because the consultee gets stuck or the consultant gets stuck in a blind alley. Hylander's theory provides many insights into best practices.

Responding to Lack of Knowledge and Lack of Skill

Table 2.1 lists Caplan's four sources of consultee difficulty, their corresponding descriptions, signs of the difficulty during consultation, and the consultant's responses to such difficulties.

TABLE 2.1 Signs and consultant responses based on Caplan's category of consultee difficulty

Consultee difficulty	Description	Signs emerging during consultation interview	Consultant response
Lack of Knowledge	Knowledge missing about psychology or pedagogy	Verbal acknowledge of ignorance. Errors in descriptions	Provide psychological knowledge to the system directly or indirectly. Offer group consultation.
Lack of Skill	Consultee understands causes of problem and principles underlying intervention but executes poorly	Skill deficits revealed in review of what has been done previously with client	Avoid assuming supervisory role. Facilitate exposure to role model.
Lack of Self-Confidence	Reluctance to engage with or change modes of working with the client	Anxiety. Avoidance	Provide peer support through group consultation. Provide nonspecific ego support.

(Continued)

TABLE 2.1 (Continued)

Consultee difficulty	Description	Signs emerging during consultation interview	Consultant response
Lack of Objectivity	Direct personal involvement	Client seems like an object for the satisfaction of personal needs	Support professional identity and ethics. Replace personal need with the satisfaction of professional goal achievement. Discuss client's parallel needs. Self-disclosure.
	Simple identification	Similarity between consultee and client. Consultee taking sides	Provide a role model by being empathetic with all relevant actors in consultation dilemma. Consider multiple perspectives.
	Transference	Consultee imposes on dilemma a pattern of roles from previous life experiences or fantasies. Strong emotion	Reality testing through careful observation. Considering a reversal of roles or cause and effect.
	Characterological distortions	Minor disorders evidenced—consultee "strange"	Support defenses and lower anxiety. Increase intellectual understanding. Remain task oriented. Group consultation.
	Theme interference	Special type of transference. Suddenly occurs in otherwise effective professional. Theme takes the form of a syllogism. Stereotyping	Demonstrate that the inevitable outcome is only one possibility. Cardinal error: Remove client from initial category.

Lack of Knowledge

Rarely are a consultee's difficulties of Caplan's first type because the consultee has absolutely no theory or conception of what is occurring. However, some consultees are completely in the dark about what is causing the client's behaviors. Others will have ideas about causes but will not know what to do. The obvious response is to arrange for the consultee to get the needed knowledge.

Whether or not the consultant supplies information or refers the consultee to other sources depends on many factors. One has to do with the organizational structure of the institution in which the consultee works. Are there in-service opportunities, curricular resources, mentors, or supervisors available to supply pedagogical knowledge? Peers are available in group consultation to supply information about educational theory and practice.

A second factor has to do with the consultant's knowledge and experience. Can the consultant impart knowledge in a way that makes it easy for consultees to apply it to their situation? Consultants should always be ready to explain aspects of psychological theory or mental health principles in simple terms. They can talk about theory and practice as applied to their own work and help consultees see the possible connection. They can also collect readings or online resources to supplement their teaching. The consultant is not presenting information to consultees in their professional domain (e.g., pedagogy), but rather the consultant's role in the partnership is to bring psychological theory, explanations, and knowledge to the conversation so they can be used in the classroom or school.

Lack of Skill

The key to responding to lack of skill in a consultee is to avoid assuming a supervisory role, but to locate and encourage the use of models with whom the consultee can identify, and who can illustrate the needed skill. The consultant can, however, provide emotional support and encourage the consultee to practice the new skill. The consultant can offer role-playing experience and provide feedback. In group consultation, peers may volunteer to serve as models or identify other resources.

Caplan's last two sources of difficulty, lack of self-confidence and lack of objectivity, are more related to affective rather than cognitive issues. Some new learning occurs from the process of responding to them, but the consultant must address emotions for this to occur.

Consultee-Centered Consultation and Emotion

Responding to feelings and emotion is another hallmark of consultee-centered consultation. Our professional identity and ability to function well in a professional role is a source of great satisfaction. Mental health and happiness, according to Freud, as reported by Erikson (1968), is dependent on our capacity to love and to work (*lieben und arbeiten*). When problems occur in a work setting, it follows that a responsible professional will feel some distress, anxiety, frustration, and anger. To ask for help with a work problem is a sign of coping, but at the same time, it may be an admission of failure. Anger is a common reaction to feelings of helplessness both inside and outside of professional roles.

Berlin wrote, "Hopefully, the consultant can also aid the teacher, under the trying conditions of very difficult classrooms, to recognize his human feelings of despair, anger, and even hate, as well as a sort of general guilt at not being able to love all the children and work miracles for them. When she or he understands these as common human feelings, the teacher often feels less frustrated and is able to work more effectively bit by bit and day by day" (Berlin, 1967, p. 38).

Much anger and frustration comes from individuals being unable to live up to unrealistic professional expectations. Parker (1962) noted that the work of pre-school teachers engendered specific attitudes and emotions, that along with common personality characteristics, lead to a number of ideas that might be addressed in consultation. The topics raised in consultation are often related to these ideas and the guilt associated with feeling angry because of these ideas. Parker's (1962, p. 560) list of common teacher beliefs follows.

1. It is unprofessional for a teacher to become angry at a child or his parent(s).
2. If you understand a problem, you should be able to solve it.
3. "Permissiveness" is good, "Authoritarianism" is bad (or vice versa).
4. A really good teacher never dislikes a child.
5. A teacher should be able to help all children who show an obvious need.
6. A prime goal of nursery school is to help all children become "integrated with the group."
7. It is an important part of the teacher's job to help parents develop "healthy relationships" with their children. To do so, the teacher's role is one of counseling with mothers and understanding their personal problems.
8. Disturbed parents and/or family relationships produce disturbed children invariably.
9. Or, a disturbed child will inevitably be found to have a disturbed family.
10. If a teacher does feel anger, dislike, or any other undesirable feeling he must at least control any recognizable expression of that feeling.

Although this list was generated from work with the teachers of very young children, it is a list that with slight modification is easily identifiable as being characteristic of many teachers and school administrators. Secondary teachers, however, probably do not hold ideas 3, 6, and 7 to a great extent. As Parker pointed out, many of these ideas are erroneous, and many are true under certain conditions but not others.

These ideas reflect the teachers' feelings that they are on their own in the classroom and should be able to handle every situation that comes their way. These self-expectations are a heavy burden to bear, and in part, are encouraged by teacher educators. Instructors in teacher education provide lectures on how to discipline and manage children and how to talk with parents. They talk from theory and provide general principles in a way that makes complex human interactions seem simple and straight-forward. The student teacher then observes a "master teacher" who is a model, experienced teacher and who makes the whole, complex process seem simple to the novice. Very seldom are the feelings that children and parents arouse in teachers discussed, and very rarely are teachers encouraged to find ways to express these feelings. If they can learn to express feelings naturally and comfortably, children can learn from them that it is permissible to express emotions and that such expression does not automatically bring about destruction and pain to others (Berlin, 1956). Teachers are not trained to ask for help, nor is the discussion of problems a routine part of the teacher's options for the day. If teaching is a lonely profession, as Sarason (1996) claims, part of this loneliness is built on self-expectations.

In Parker's list, ideas 1, 4, and 10 all seem to be related to the estrangement of the teacher from emotion and feelings. Consultants need to be aware that consultees will have a great deal of difficulty recognizing the frustration and anger they feel toward children and parents. To the extent they believe these are unprofessional feelings they will be reluctant to be open about them.

Ideas 2, 5, 6, and to some extent 3, betray how teachers have unrealistic expectations for what they can do with children in their classrooms, which is coupled with a lack of appreciation for individual differences in children. These notions imply a belief that there is one correct way of doing a thing or single way to solve all problems. The consultant must also be aware of the strong feelings that teachers have that there are magical ways of working with others that will be immediately successful, if only one knew about them. When the consultant does not deliver this information, the consultant may be perceived as withholding and perversely uncooperative.

Ideas 7, 8, and 9 are related to attitudes about family dynamics and classroom behavior, which are greatly oversimplified. It is clear that family dynamics do play a role in children's adjustment to school, but the invariability of these relationships is a myth. This belief may be a source of many themes consultants will need to address in consultation.

Consultation Processes for Addressing Emotion and Facilitating Emotional Discharge

General Approach

Based on his experience, Berlin has outlined six steps in his consultation process (Berlin, 2001). Most of these steps are designed to respond to the consultee's emotions.

1. Assess the conflicts between consultee and client that result in the consultee's anxieties and troubles with the client.
2. Assess the consultee's strengths that have enabled him or her to work effectively.
3. Reduce the consultee's tension and feelings of failure by comments communicating understanding, sympathy, and acceptance of the consultee's problems. The consultant can often describe similar problems the consultant has encountered, thus delineating these as professional problems.
4. Describe feelings similar to those of the consultee in the face of similar client behavior.
5. Decide on a course of action and follow-up to evaluate, communicating confidence in the consultee.

Responding to Consultee Lack of Self-Confidence and Lack of Objectivity

Caplan also discussed managing affective issues, but in the context of sources of consultee difficulty. He argued against lowering anxiety through reassurance, since this will foster dependence on the consultant. Instead, by jointly examining the facts of the case and sharing concern, the consultant will provide ego support. "If the consultee feels that the consultant has truly understood the intricacies of the case and takes the client's predicament seriously, and yet remains professionally calm, he will identify with these attitudes, and his own anxiety level and fear for the client will be reduced" (Caplan & Caplan, 1993, p. 68).

Lack of Self-confidence

Often a consultee will have the knowledge and skill necessary to address the problem but will be reluctant to proceed. For example, a skilled teacher who has been successful with Anglo children may be reluctant to implement a valid strategy with an African American child. Some reluctance may be justified, but after taking cultural issues into account, the consultant may supply needed nonspecific ego support. Simply discussing the cultural issues objectively may be sufficient. Consultants are supportive by being empathetic listeners and responding verbally and nonverbally with calmness and optimism. The consultant can probe for mistaken ideas and fears, so they may be examined by testing them against reality. A comment such as "what is the worst thing that can happen" encourages the consultee to recognize that many fears are groundless. Attending carefully to issues of treatment acceptability is particularly important. In group consultation peers can also provide encouragement and help the consultee believe that an intervention they are considering has a reasonable probability of success.

Lack of Objectivity

When a consultee has no conceptualization or a naïve, but not strongly held, idea about the causes of the problem with a client, the issue is lack of knowledge.

However, a consultee may have a conceptualization that is clouded by per, subjective factors, that is emotionally charged, and that leads to the consultee bei, professionally too close or too distant from the client's situation. These clients lack objectivity. As listed in Table 2.1 overlapping categories include (a) direct personal involvement, (b) simple identification, (c) transference, (d) characterological distortions, and (e) theme interference. The table includes suggestions for addressing each.

Direct Personal Involvement

A consultee looses objectivity when he or she shifts from a professional relationship with the client to a personal one. Teachers often assume a parental role with students and sometimes a romantic one. Caplan's solution is to help the consultee replace the satisfaction of a personal need with the satisfaction of achieving professional goals. One way to accomplish this is by discussing how the client is getting personal needs met by the consultee and yet needs to get these same needs met in other, more natural ways, typically by academic success or improved family or peer relationships. Alternatively, Caplan suggests the consultant can model attending empathetically to the needs of the client and at the same time maintain emotional distance.

Simple identification. Consultees can also get into trouble by identifying with the client or with others in the client's life such as the parents. Different from transference, simple identification is stimulated by obvious similarity between the consultee and client. These similarities make it easier for the consultee to make unwarranted assumptions. Identification may occur when the consultee and client are of the same ethnicity or background. In simple identification, the consultee often will take sides with some actors in the problem.

Again, the consultant responds by modeling an empathetic but neutral approach to all of the actors in the situation. The consultant and consultee jointly examine all of the details of the client's behavior, avoiding biases.

Transference. Transference differs from simple identification in that consultees impose thoughts and feelings from their own life experiences on to the client and other participants in the consultation problem. The consultee brings emotionally charged attitudes, perceptions, expectations, and set judgments to examining the client's situation. These fantasies often impede rational objective analysis and action.

The consultant responds to transference distortions by encouraging reality testing. By having the consultee examine objective data about behavior, his or her expectations can change. The consultant can also mention alternative explanations for behavior in the spirit of examining all possibilities.

Characterological distortions. Some consultees will have minor emotional disturbances that will not be serious enough to generally affect work performance, although others will perceive them as a bit strange or irritating. Consultants can help by supporting the consultee's coping mechanisms and reducing anxiety by nonverbal acceptance and increasing professional distance from clients.

Theme interference. Caplan is best known for his thoughts on theme interference reduction. However, he acknowledged that many consultants, particularly school-based practitioners, have not endorsed this technique (Caplan, Caplan, & Erchul, 1995). A theme is "a conflict related to actual life experience or to fantasies that has not been satisfactorily resolved (and that) is apt to persist in a consultee's preconscious or unconscious as an emotionally toned cognitive constellation" (Caplan & Caplan, 1993, p. 122). Caplan suggested that in many cases, themes interfere with effective problem solving and are more difficult to address because of the negative affect. He described how themes may be understood as syllogisms the consultee has constructed consisting of an initial category and an inevitable outcome. In consultation, these themes must be shown to be inadequate before new ways of working with and conceptualizing the client can emerge. Theme interference techniques include (a) demonstrating that the inevitable outcome is only one logical possibility and that other outcomes are more likely than the dreaded one, and (b) avoiding giving nonverbal validation to the theme outcome. These techniques of theme interference reduction are attempts at conceptual change inasmuch as they attempt to influence syllogisms constructed by the consultee. They contribute to prevention by reducing the chance the theme will be applied to future clients.

Instead of offering a completely different conceptualization, however, the aim of consultee-centered consultation is to elaborate the theme in such a way to make membership in the initial category imply a number of different outcomes and to complicate the picture. The resulting changed syllogism will suggest that many outcomes are possible and that none are inevitable. The revised theme will be more plausible and fruitful for working with other clients. One approach is to bring in anomalous data to indicate how the initial category did not lead to the inevitable outcome. As Caplan suggested, the emphasis should be on how the initial theory is inadequate, not on how the theory is inapplicable to the particular client; that is, by removing the client from the initial category. There will be no motive to change the theory if it is perceived as not applying to the client.

Stages of Consultation

Consultation is a fluid process involving a conversation or dialogue between the participants. Since it has a purpose and is time limited, there usually is a common progression through a series of stages and activities. The progression is not necessarily linear, as there may be some back and forth through the stages.

There seems to be consensus among scholars that there are at least five stages common to all models of school-based consultation: (a) Relationship building, (b) Problem identification, (c) Problem analysis, (d) Intervention implementation, and (e) Program evaluation (Kratochwill, Elliott, & Rotto, 1995).

To understand the consultee-centered consultation approach it is useful to break these stages down more completely. Davis and I (Sandoval & Davis, 1984) incorporated the ideas of Berlin (1967, 1977) and Caplan (1970) into an eight-step process-oriented model. The result is the following.

Step 1. Orientation, Relationship Building, and Maintaining rapport—Work at establishing and maintaining a strong collaborative, task-oriented working relationship. At the same time reduce the consultee's anxieties and self-doubts by emphatic listening and understanding.

Step 2. Problem Exploration, Definition, and Reframing—Develop a working hypothesis about what the problem(s) or difficulties seem to be. Analyze the client's current behavior and the consultee's response. Review what has been tried: Inquire about what has already transpired with the client; that is, what has been tried with what level of success has been achieved with this client and others. Determine who else has been asked for help. Generate alternative explanations for the problem.

Step 3. Gather Data as Needed—Collect information from the client or others in the client's or consultee's systems. Gather information about the client's background and community.

Step 4. Share Information and Hypothesis Generation and Reframing—Share obtained data or other information with the consultee to complete a new or amplified view of the client and the consultee's system.

Step 5. Analyze Systemic Forces—Consider the cultural, institutional, and idiosyncratic pressures impinging on the problem.

Step 6. Generate Interventions—Collaboratively develop approaches to or interventions for the "problem" while promoting consultee independence and confidence. Brainstorm alternative strategies. Specify consultee and consultant responsibilities.

Step 7. Supporting Experiments and Interventions—Support the actions of the consultee as necessary.

Step 8. Follow-up and Disengagement—Plan for follow-up, which includes reevaluation and revision of interventions if necessary. If successful, review problem resolution for education of consultee; if unsuccessful, return to step 2 or 3 depending on the level of rapport with the consultee, or terminate consultation.

The following eight chapters will expand on what occurs in each of these steps. The steps can be characterized by the frequency of use of various modes of interaction as described by Hylander (2004, 2012), and by how the consultant responds to learning needs and emotions.

Guidelines for Consultants

Each of the eight chapters will conclude with a set of guidelines to help the consultant reflect on what has occurred during the particular step in the consultation process. Consultants need to constantly monitor their behavior if they are to improve as professionals.

First will come *Interpersonal-Behavioral* guidelines. These are the actions and strategies used by the consultant to accomplish the goals of each step. Included second will be *Interpersonal-Cognitive* guidelines, which are intended to catalog the work of the consultant in thinking over issues of importance and generating an approach to the problem. Finally will come sample *Self-Guiding* questions. These questions are intended to get the consultant thinking about the predominant issues and goals of that particular step. The answers to the questions help the consultant to decide how to proceed. They are also test questions for the consultant to use in monitoring ongoing effectiveness.

Beginning consultants may use these guidelines to manage the consultation process. Consultation proceeds by the consultant asking him or herself questions, attending to the answers, formulating approaches and hypotheses, and implementing those approaches considered most appropriate. In an experienced consultant this self-questioning likely becomes unconscious and automatic, but for those starting out, this practice of explicit question–asking appears most helpful.

References

Berlin, I. N. (1956). Some learning experiences as psychiatric consultant in schools. *Mental Hygiene, 40*, 215–236.

Berlin, I.N. (1966). Transference and countertransference in community psychiatry. *Archives of General Psychiatry, 15,* 165–172.

Berlin, I. N. (1967). Preventive aspects of mental health consultation to schools. *Mental Hygiene, 51*, 34–40.

Berlin, I. N. (1977). Some lessons learned in 25 years of mental health consultation to schools. In S.C. Plog & P.I. Ahmed (Eds.), *Principles and techniques of mental health consultation* (pp. 23–48). New York: Plenum Publishing Corporation.

Berlin, I.N. (2001). A retrospective view of school mental health consultation. *Child and Adolescent Psychiatric Clinics of North America, 12,* 25–31.

Caplan, G. (1963). Types of mental health consultation. *American Journal of Orthopsychiatry, 33,* 470–481.

Caplan, G. (1970). *The theory and practice of mental health consultation.* New York: Basic Books.

Caplan, G., & Caplan, R.B. (1993). *The theory and practice of mental health consultation.* San Francisco: Jossey-Bass.

Caplan, G., Caplan, R.B., & Erchul, W.P. (1995). A contemporary view of mental health consultation: Comments on "Types of mental health consultation" by Gerald Caplan (1963). *Journal of Educational and Psychological Consultation, 6,* 23–30.

Cobern, W.W. (1993). Constructivism. *Journal of Educational and Psychological Consultation, 4,* 105–112.

Erikson, E.H. (1968). *Identity, youth and crisis,* New York: W.W. Norton.

Henning-Stout, M. (1994). Consultation and connected knowing: What we know is determined by the questions we ask. *Journal of Educational and Psychological Consultation, 5,* 5–21.

Hylander, I. (2000). *Turning processes. The change of representations in consultee-centered case consultation* (Dissertation). Linköping: Linköping University.

Hylander, I. (2004). Analysis of conceptual change in consultee-centered consultation. In N. M. Lambert, I. Hylander, & J. H. Sandoval (Eds.), *Consultee-centered consultation,* (pp.45–61). Mahwah, NJ: Lawrence Erlbaum.

Hylander, I. (2012). Conceptual change through consultee-centered consultation: A theoretical model. *Consulting Psychology Journal: Practice and Research, 64,* 29–45.

Kratochwill, T.R., Elliott, S.N., & Rotto, P.C. (1995). Best practices in school-based behavioral consultation. In A. Thomas & J. Grimes (Eds.), *Best practices in school psychology III* (pp. 519–535). Bethesda, MD: NASP.

Kuhn, T. S. (1962). *The structure of scientific revolutions.* Chicago: University of Chicago Press.

Parker, B. (1962). Some observations on psychiatric consultation with nursery school teachers. *Mental Hygiene, 46,* 559–566.

Posner, G.P., Strike, K.A., Hewson, P.W., & Gertzog, W.A. (1982). Accommodation of a scientific conception: Toward a theory of conceptual change. *Science Education, 66,* 211–227.

Sandoval, J., & Davis, J.M. (1984). A school-based mental health consultation curriculum. *Journal of School Psychology, 22,* 31–43.

Sarason, S. B. (1996). *Revisiting "The culture of the school and the problem of change."* New York: Teachers College Press.

Van der Veer, R., & Valsiner, J. (1991). *Understanding Vygotsky: A quest for synthesis.* Oxford: Basil Blackwell.

3

BUILDING A CONSULTATION RELATIONSHIP AND MAINTAINING RAPPORT

The aim of this chapter is to present some specific skills and procedures for entering into a nonhierarchical consultation relationship with teachers, administrators, parents, or others with whom the mental health worker might wish to consult. Specific skills include (a) establishing proximity, (b) dealing with expectations, and (c) establishing rapport through empathetic listening. But first, the school-based consultant must obtain sanction from superiors and peers in the educational system to provide consultation as part of his or her duties.

Negotiating a Role with Administrators

Caplan, as a consultant from an outside agency, devotes a chapter in his book to this issue (Caplan & Caplan, 1993). However as a school-based internal consultant, there are different issues to address in negotiating a consultation role. Internal consultants will have to convince site-level and district-level administrators that in the consultant they have an untapped resource.

School administrators may hold the view that school psychologists only serve the special education process, or that school counselors and social workers should spend all of their time with children and parents. And indeed much of their time *will* be in providing direct services. Nevertheless, administrators and others need to know the full extent of the services mental health professionals can provide in the school and their value. With experience they should be able to appreciate the value of early intervention through consultation to prevent problems from requiring a more expensive and time-consuming intervention or special education.

In spite of being a part of the institution, it may be necessary to argue and demonstrate that the time a school psychologist, social worker, or counselor spends consulting is valuable and contributes as much to the mission of the school as other activities, such as working directly with pupils. School-based mental health professionals must present themselves as being trained and having the expectation that, at least part of the time, they will function as consultants to the adults in the system. This effort will involve constantly educating others in the institution about your professional knowledge and skills, and displaying them.

Local evaluations of consultation are important tools for demonstrating the utility of consultation. By collecting concrete, data-based evidence that consultation activities are met by consultee usage and satisfaction, that special education referrals are reduced but more needy students are served, that student disciplinary actions are reduced, and that children are meeting academic goals, administrators can, over time, come to see consultation as a valuable service. Zins (1981) reported using evaluative data to influence administrators to permit consultation service to grow from one hour per week to the majority of services provided by school-based consultants. School-based mental health consultants must be prepared to demonstrate that their consultation role benefits the children of the school.

Assuming administrators are willing, the consultant must set up a number of agreements with administrators before a program of consultation begins at a school site. They may jointly set up procedural guidelines to specify:

1. How children will become the subject of consultation conversations.
2. How much time will be spent on consultation for an individual child.
3. What limits there might be on working outside of the special education system and when it will be important to move into a consideration of a special education intervention.
4. How the process will normally be considered to transpire. For example, it will almost always involve problem definition, intervention planning, and follow up and evaluation.
5. The need for confidentiality and its limits.
6. How the program of consultation will be evaluated.
7. What motives or values the consultant may have that might lead to unsanctioned change or otherwise conflict with values held by other personnel. (Hughes, 1986)

Administrators also need to be willing to support teacher consultees by providing sanction and time during the workday for meetings with the consultant to take place. They must actively endorse the process, encourage subordinates to seek consultation, and not undermine the consultant by making conflicting demands on teachers or otherwise interfering with the process.

Some administrators may believe that the consultant is appropriating one of their valued roles, that of supporting and supervising their staff. They may even resent the time consultants have to speak with teachers. It will be important for administrators to appreciate the difference between consultation and supervision and that the consultant is bringing different expertise to the table during consultation. Teachers will still benefit from the administrator's mentorship and supervision as an experienced educational leader. The intent is for consultants to supplement, not replace, the administrator's role in helping teachers and children.

In addition, others in the system, such as principals and superintendents who have a supervisory role, may ask the consultant for evaluative information about consultees' work with clients and not respect the consultant's need to maintain confidentially. They may ask a consultant to initiate consultation with a teacher they are supervising, particularly if they sense the teacher is not performing well and they do not have the time or inclination to intervene. Consultants must be clear that their job is to be of help. They should inform their supervisors that their expertise draws from psychology not teaching, that consultation is voluntary, and that it is inappropriate to report back on what occurs during consultation. The previously mentioned features are what makes consultation work. At the same time, they must encourage and help the supervisor to do his or her job effectively. That job involves mentoring and evaluation, neither of which is part of the consultation role. Issues of confidentiality, particularly, will have to be clarified and acknowledged with the supervisor prior to the initiation of consultation (Brown, Pryzwansky, & Schulte, 2011). Consultants must be able to explain to administrators the constraints on consultation as well as the benefits.

Establishing Proximity

Whether or not the request for help turns into a request for consultation depends a lot on how the teacher or other consultee views the consultant. Consultation involves a working relationship and the consultant will need to be seen as trustworthy, empathetic, and competent. There are three steps to creating a dynamic, productive relationship: establishing proximity, dealing with expectations, and listening empathetically.

It may be obvious but the first step in consultation is being available to the consultee. If the consultant is busy with other roles, such as testing children for special education eligibility or doing college counseling with students, teachers will view mental health professionals as only providing direct services to children and not indirect services to adults. It is an error to only interact with potential consultees in the context of case work. Potential consultees need to see the school psychologist, social worker, or counselor interacting positively with adults as well as children and feel that they have access to their time. Although school-based consultants may have other duties that occupy them, it is still important to make time to be with the staff of the school and join them in both professional and social pursuits. It will take time for them to get used to and comfortable with a new consultant. The consultant needs to be approachable and use normal conversational gambits to start conversations with potential consultees when meeting them casually in the school setting. Consultants need to spend time in the teacher's workroom, on the playground, in the school office, or other locations where

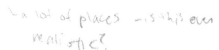
a lot of places — is this even realistic?

potential consultants congregate. They need to be friendly and initially find ways to help out with the general mission of the school. They need to be willing to roll up their sleeves and participate in school activities including special events. Often initial requests for assistance will be for trivial matters; nevertheless, these will be opportunities to prove a willingness to help as well as trustworthiness as a member of the team. For example a teacher on yard duty might ask the consultant to watch a group of children while she or he is occupied elsewhere. Or a principal might ask the consultant to monitor a group test or chaperon a dance. There are, of course, limits to the consultant's willingness to volunteer. The tasks they take on should be of short duration, should assist but not substitute for another's normal duties, and should be consistent with professionalism. If the consultant agrees to do something, he or she must follow through and keep the commitment. By completing tasks cheerfully, accurately, and on time, the consultant builds trust. Of course by performing the consultant's normal duties such as direct services to children in a responsible, professional, and competent manner equally demonstrates integrity.

Although it is important not to be viewed as a gossip, the consultant should not be overly guarded. It is appropriate to disclose personal information or opinions, always keeping confidentiality in mind. A useful principle in offering information or an opinion is to be brief and invite a response from the listener. In this way the consultant will not be seen as a lecturer or egotistical bloviator.

It will also be important to conform to the local culture of the school. The consultant should dress professionally but follow any traditions established in the setting. Both grooming and dress need to communicate professionalism and stability. If there are staff social events during or after school, the consultant should consider participating. The goal is to be perceived as part of the group, even though the consultant may not be present on site every day.

It is also vital for the consultant to be aware of stereotypes about mental health professionals. Some of these stereotypes involve eccentric behavior, being analytical and critical of what others say and do, and being distant. Often when walking into a school the staff might say, "the shrink is here." It is important to respond and make clear that the consultant is not engaging in psychoanalysis or otherwise being judgmental of staff members.

Becoming perceived as trustworthy and as a part of a team may take longer in multicultural settings (Gibbs, 1980). The consultant will have to work through cultural beliefs that may exist about other groups. Some of the stereotypes that may exist will have to do with cultural insensitivity or cultural bias. Until potential consultees have had an opportunity to witness unbiased behavior in cultural exchanges, they will remain suspicious.

The goal of establishing proximity is to provide an opportunity for conversation between the consultant and consultee "in a setting where it is socially acceptable for them to talk informally without significant commitment on either side. In this situation, the consultant should appear approachable, and should perhaps initiate the contact with some informal bridge comments about the weather or questions about the institution" (Caplan & Caplan, 1993, p. 62). During initial conversations the consultant demonstrates friendliness, interest in the consultee and the problems of clients, and lack of malice. "The consultant's job is to demonstrate that he is not seductive or critical, will not attack defenses, and will not uncover weakness or unacceptable thoughts" (Caplan & Caplan, 1993, pp. 62–63). These initial conversations can lead directly to requests for consultation.

Who Initiates Consultation?

Consultee-centered consultation is voluntary. However, either the consultee, the consultant, or a third person might initiate the process. It is most clearly voluntary when the consultee makes a request to meet about a client or other problem. Typically, such a request comes after a consultant has proved to be competent and trustworthy in other roles in the school. If the consultant has established proximity, conversations can begin easily.

Consultants can also initiate consultation by issuing an open invitation to potential consultees. They might indicate their availability through a formal presentation to the staff or proceed on a case-by-case basis. The stimulus for the invitation might come from working with a child or parent in a direct service role in a consultee's classroom, from informal observations of children or classrooms, or from other sources. For example, school archival data, such as disciplinary referrals, test scores, or changes in family status of children, often come to a consultant's attention from being present and involved in the school. The consultant presents the invitation tentatively but warmly and confidently. If the consultee does not accept the invitation, the consultant does not insist.

A third person might suggest consultation to either the consultee or the consultant. If the consultant has been successful, he or she may gain a positive reputation in a school, and peers may inform others of the service. The consultant may not be aware this is occurring but by being known as helpful in the consultant and other roles, the consultant becomes an important resource to the school.

A former or current consultee may also contact the consultant to identify a peer who may wish for assistance in thinking about a problem. After determining possible motivations behind such a request, the consultant might approach the potential consultee and offer to do mutual problem solving. However, keep in mind that some referrals from peers may not be benign, and instead may mask hostility and malice either toward the consultant or peer.

As mentioned before, a supervisor might also suggest consultation to his or her supervisee, or ask the consultant to initiate consultation with the supervisee. As long as consultation remains voluntary, and all understand and adhere to confidentiality, consultation may be productive.

Dealing with Expectations

In spite of efforts to educate the consultee in advance, the new consultee will be wary of the consultant and cautious in revealing their thoughts. The consultants who are new to a situation and beginning work with a new consultee or group of consultees will often face a test to determine if they can be trusted. Usually, consultees will bring up their most extreme problem in the first consultation session. There are two reasons for this phenomenon. First, the most difficult cases with the most extreme behavior are the most salient in the teacher's mind. There is a common belief that if the major problem is solved the remaining problems in the classroom will be easier. Usually this is not the case, as the next problem assumes the psychological space occupied by the previous one.

The second reason for this occurrence is to put the consultant in his or her place, to make them feel the same sense of frustration as the consultee. Misery loves company. If the consultant fails quickly to come up with a viable solution, the consultee may feel validated and justified in abandoning responsibility for the client.

If the consultant is new to the school, they may be subject to what Kelly (1993) called the second and third Caplan Laws of Consultation. The second law is "Managing the consultant's entry involves dissipating stereotypes." Consultants must identify and dissipate preconceived stereotypes on the part of the consultee and consultant. Many of these stereotypes stimulate anxiety. Kelly listed four concerns consultees have about mental health professionals: (a) the consultant can actually read their minds and will be a therapist for them, (b) the consultant will require the consultee to express innermost thoughts and feelings, (c) the consultant will not keep confidences, and (d) work colleagues will view you as being weak and incompetent if you meet with a consultant who is a "shrink." The consultant must be prepared to address these fears directly or indirectly through establishing a quality working relationship focused on the client and work problems. The focus on the client indicates a friendly alliance with the consultee and a concern and respect for the client. This dissipation of stereotypes will take time and care.

Caplan and Caplan (1993) cautioned the consultant to beware of anything that can be interpreted as being judgmental of the consultee's work, either positive or negative. Even positive complements carry the implication of the consultant being evaluative. Whenever the consultee mentions an obvious ineffectual professional behavior, the consultant remains nonjudgmental and focuses on the client.

Kelly's third law is "The first consultee who agrees to meet with the consultant is a deviant member of the organization." Kelly claimed that the first person meeting with the consultant does not share the modal values within the school. The first consultee may be *more* caring or *more* concerned about work problems than others in the school. Or the first consultee may be new to the school or an outsider in other ways. The challenge is to support this deviant consultee without reducing access to other teachers. The consultant must demonstrate commitment to the consultee and to the entire school at the same time. One way to demonstrate this, Kelly suggested, is to invite other potential consultees in similar roles or who are experiencing difficulties to meet with the consultant and the first consultee.

Starting the Conversation

Responding to Expectations for Consultation and Establishing a Contract

There are some hazards to performing multiple roles in the educational system. Because consultants may also have a direct service role (assessment, counseling), consultees may expect these services for clients when they request consultation. The consultant will need to deal with any such expectations and clarify their role.

Most consultants develop a script for explaining consultation to the consultee before the process begins and in response to a request. The script includes the goal of the process, the logistics, and the process itself. A statement about the goal might be something like, "Let's think about this problem together. Perhaps we can come up with some new ideas about how to address what is occurring in the classroom. This is a difficult situation and we may need to collect more information to decide the best course of action. But we should be able to come up with ways to address the issue."

A discussion of logistics would address both the time and location of the consultation. A consultant might say, "Let's get together after school in your classroom to discuss this situation without interruption." The consultant will wish to ask the consultee when they are available and where they would like to conduct the consultation meeting.

Discussing the duration of consultation in advance may be difficult. One of the most common expectations with which the consultant must deal is the wish for an immediate solution. It is important, somehow, for the consultant to acknowledge that human problems are difficult to solve and that it may take time to find the best approach to address the consultation dilemma. The expectation that the consultant will be able to offer a quick solution to a problem after hearing only a minimum amount of information is unrealistic. The consultant him or herself may also have some unrealistic expectations for themselves and feel pressure to respond with a quick solution to a question the consultee may have. By responding too hastily, the consultant may reinforce this idea.

The issue of confidentiality should also be explicitly addressed. The consultant must let the consultee know that what is discussed in consultation will not be revealed by the consultant. The consultee may share what occurs in consultation with others, but the consultant may not. The consultee must know that the consultant will not be reporting consultee problems to a supervisor or discussing the client's situation with other teachers or parents. However, the consultant does have an obligation to break confidentiality if there is a perceived danger to a client or consultee. Should this occur, which is rare (Caplan & Caplan, 1993), the consultant should discuss the breaking of confidentiality in advance with the consultee and supply an explanation of the consultant's reasons for taking this step.

Hughes (1986) provided an example of something a consultee-centered consultant might adapt to say to an individual consultee or to a faculty group: "I realize that the type of consultation I am offering is time-consuming for you and for me. You might wonder why I don't just test the child, interview you, perhaps observe the child in your classroom, and then recommend some approaches to you. Well, for one thing, my recommendations have a good chance of being the wrong solution to the wrong problem if I do it on my own. Also, I hope that by involving you in jointly exploring the problem and generating solutions, you will find yourself better prepared to cope with similar problems in the future, without my help. I hope I can help you prevent children's problems by enlarging upon your already considerable skills" (Hughes, 1986, p. 493).

Preparing Teachers and Other Consumers of Consultation

Although it is true that the special services worker is largely responsible for guiding the process of consultation, the teacher also has some process responsibilities and can be informed about them to enhance the process. Teachers need to learn at least four concepts (Sandoval, Lambert, & Davis, 1977).

First they need to learn what it is they are free to discuss with the consultant, that is, that they are to discuss job related problems they are having with children or others. They must know what the "contract" is with the consultant. They must discover that consultation is not supervision or psychotherapy and that the content is restricted to work-related situations.

Second, they must learn to participate in the consultation process. They need to understand that the consultant will ask questions, and will attempt to understand the problem as clearly and exhaustively as possible. As a result, the teacher must gain skill and confidence in presenting a problem for discussion or consideration.

Third they must come to understand the nature of suggestion and experimentation. As ideas are generated about possible solutions, the teacher has to learn that they are suggestions for experiments in the classroom. They must realize that they may reject ideas and that they are offered in the spirit of brainstorming. Suggestions are not mandates or advice that must be followed. Also, a suggestion is not a solution but rather something to try and later to evaluate. The consultee must come to appreciate that suggestions are genuine contributions for discussion rather than insults to the individual's professional intelligence and integrity.

Finally, teachers must accept that he or she must act. That is, the teacher has responsibility for making changes in the student's experience and the act of seeking consultation is not an act of giving over responsibility or authority to another person.

Essentially, it is helpful to the process if the consultee forms realistic expectations for consultation. It is possible to inform consultees about appropriate expectations directly and to do so is more efficient than having them learn through protracted interactions with consultants.

Establishing Rapport

Responding to Content: Active Listening

When the consultee finally approaches the consultant for help or consultation, the consultant responds by active listening. The consultant lets the consultee tell their story and facilitates the telling by both verbal and nonverbal means. One way to facilitate the story is to help the consultee pace the delivery of the information. Some interruptions are acceptable in order to slow the consultee down and help them organize their thoughts. These interruptions should take place at natural points in the conversation and may consist of questions or comments.

Caplan advised, "I do not allow the consultee to talk for more than a few minutes without interrupting him with a question. I avoid, under all circumstances, a situation in which I listen in relative silence while the consultee tells a long story about the client and then turns to me and says 'what do you think about it and what should I do?' First, I probably will not know what he should do. Second, since I may not yet know what the elements in the story really mean to the consultee, I risk saying something that has an inner meaning to the consultee. Third, by then my silence will have allowed the consultee to develop doubts about my attitude to him" (Caplan & Caplan, 1993, pp. 64–65).

At the beginning of the conversation the consultant's goal is to make responses that are interchangeable with what the consultee has said. This practice is to communicate empathy and understanding. The counseling techniques of restatement and summarization may be used to good effect. Courses in counseling typically teach these techniques. Restatement involves repeating the consultee's actual words back to him or her, or repeating portions of what the consultee has said. The idea is to give the consultee an opportunity to correct what you have selected and also to elaborate. Paraphrasing, in contrast, is capturing the meaning of the consultee's statement but in different words. Summarization involves providing the consultee with an overview of what they have told you, again providing them with an opportunity to correct your version of what you have heard. In each case it is important to provide an accuracy check. The accuracy check may be communicated by tone of voice, a rising inflection suggesting a question mark, or a verbal statement of something like "is that right?" or "have I got it?"

The purpose of these responses is to assure the consultee that the consultant understands the situation from the consultee's point of view. To use Hylander's term, the consultation is in the approach mode with the goal of listening to the consultee's presentation and comprehending the consultee's conception or representation of the problem.

Responding to Feelings

A major tenet of consultee-centered consultation is that there is almost always anxiety, anger, and guilt present in the consultation conversation coming from not being able to solve a professional problem. Moreover the consultee may be unable to admit to such feelings easily, since they are viewed as unprofessional. However consultees experience a great deal of relief when they find a place where they can safely express their emotions.

The major techniques for dealing with feelings when they are present in the consultation setting are through both nonverbal and verbal acceptance. The consultant must acknowledge the feelings as feelings and remain nonjudgmental.

Nonverbal Response to Feelings

Nonverbal techniques include maintaining a neutral facial expression and a relaxed body posture during the initial description of the consultation difficulty. This is not to say one neglects feelings but rather responds to them symbolically by remaining calm and unexcited, implying that the emotions are acceptable and normal under the circumstances. Of course it is also so important to acknowledge positive feelings as well. In fact it is possible for the consultee to have both positive and negative feelings about the same client.

Some other important nonverbal behavior that facilitates communication is the body position of the consultant and the consultee. Being squarely oriented to the consultee, facing them with the consultant's shoulders parallel to the consultee's shoulders, communicates that the consultant is attending closely and is not looking away or being distracted. In addition keeping an open stance, that is, avoiding crossing one's arms and one's legs, is also important in indicating openness to listening to other's opinions rather than defensiveness. Other body language that communicates the consultant is attending is leaning forward as opposed to leaning backward. Eye contact is also important. Although there are some cultural situations in which eye contact is not desirable, in general looking someone in the eye communicates both honesty and that the listener is paying attention. During the consultation conversation keeping one's muscles relaxed and a facial expression neutral suggests that the consultant is listening carefully, but moreover is not shocked or disturbed by what the consultee is saying. It may seem contradictory to assume a relaxed posture while at the same time being attentive, but the right balance may be achieved.

Having the right setting is also important. Consultation should take place in a location and at a time when others will not interrupt. It should also be free from distractions and take place when other obligations are not pressing. The setting should allow for a confidential conversation to take place. Empty classrooms, private offices or out-of-doors alone are possiblities. It may be difficult to find these settings in the school environment, nevertheless, having a comfortable place to work will be important.

Verbal Response to Feelings

The consultant's major response to feelings is through the technique of reflection. The consultant attends to what is being said and either restates the feeling or summarizes feelings that the consultee has expressed. If the consultee has not been explicit, the consultant may ask about feelings; for example, "How did you feel when your client did that?" or "You must have been pleased when your client asked for help." For a review of ways to respond, the reader is referred to Egan's well-known text (2009).

Responding to Questions from the Consultee

At some point the consultee may ask the consultant what he or she thinks about what has been said. Of course the consultant must respond, but not always right away. First the consultant must be sure he or she has understood the question. One way to make sure is to repeat the question or rephrase it before responding and to allow the consultee to correct you if you have missed the point. Another technique is playing for time by gathering more information before responding. A consultant might say, "I will answer your question, but first I must know . . ." This will be useful if it is not perceived as evasive. If the request is for simple information, answer quickly.

One response to a question is to return it back to the consultee, for example, "What possibilities occur to you?" Answering a question with a question is a stereotyped response and should be employed minimally. A better alternative may be to answer *first,* then invite the consultee to respond to the same question.

Consultants should be sensitive to general or abstract questions and turn them into specific or concrete questions by asking, "Do you have a specific situation in mind?" (Altrocchi, 1972).

The consultee may ask about others with whom the consultee works. Questions such as this may raise the issue of confidentiality and the consultant must respond in a way that indicates that confidential information must remain confidential. The consultant explains that he or she cannot talk about others just as he or she cannot talk about the consultee with others.

In all responses to questions the consultant attempts to be helpful to the consultee, is honest and sensitive when he or she answers (and also when he or she cannot answer), and returns the focus of the consultation back to the work relationship with the client (Benjamin, 1969).

Using and Responding to Consultee Silence

Silence is not necessarily to be avoided in consultation. The use of silence on the part of the consultant is relative to each conversation's tempo and patterns of speech. Some consultees will pause and be silent for relatively long periods of time. The consultant must judge whether or not to also remain silent in order to give the consultees an opportunity to think or get their thoughts together. Long silences, however, may suggest that the consultee is waiting for a response from the consultant. The consultant may be tempted to fill the silence with anything that comes to mind, because many silences are uncomfortable. However the consultant should use silence as an opportunity to collect his or her own thoughts and to direct the interview appropriately. Again during silences the consultant should remain alert and through facial expression and body language communicate thoughtfulness and interest.

Responding to Complements

One of the hallmarks of consultee-centered consultation is that there is a nonhierarchical relationship between the consultant and the consultee. The ideal is for two professionals coming from different fields to solve the problem jointly drawing on the unique expertise of each. To maintain a relationship with equal status the consultant must respond to certain of the consultee's statements with *one-downsmanship*. This technique involves being aware when the consultee is elevating the consultant to a superior status, or is denigrating the consultee's own expertise or skill. The consultant should be prepared to react either to compliments and praise directed at them, or to the consultee's statements of self deprecation, false modesty, or self-criticism.

When this occurs, consultants respond by being purposely modest about themselves, and at the same time, complimentary about the consultee. The consultant must be prepared to resist attempts to elevate his or her status by pointing out valuable skills and knowledge possessed by the consultee. For example, if the teacher flatters the consultant about an idea, the consultant might reply that the teacher will know best how to use or modify the idea in the classroom. Another response to consultee attempts to raise the status of the consultant and become dependent is to practice self-disclosure about one's own shortcomings in doing professional work. When the consultee is revealing their self-shortcomings it seems only fair to reciprocate. One effect of self-disclosure is to give the consultee permission to view failure as an opportunity to reflect upon and learn from a difficult experience. The consultant's self-disclosure should include an example of sober self-reflection and the learning that has resulted from it.

Cultural Issues in Building and Maintaining Relationships

There will be cultural influences on the dynamics of the consultation conversation. The similarity or dissimilarity between the consultant and the consultee will be very important and needs to be taken into account. The consultant and consultee may be of different genders, different cultural backgrounds, and different ages, and may have wildly different experiences. It is an open question whether consultation is easier when the two participants are matched on these variables. Consultation may be easier because of shared assumptions and values that may come with similarity. However with sensitivity to differences and by sharing perspectives, consultation may result in more creative solutions when the participants are from different backgrounds. These differences will expand the universe of possibilities open to the problem-solving process.

Ingraham (2000) discussed the consultation constellation triad focusing on the cultural match between consultant, consultee, and client as well as issues when all three share a common minority culture. When the consultant and consultee are similar in background but the client is of a different cultural group, often the consultee lacks cultural information and may adopt a "color blind" approach, treating all individuals the same regardless of culture, or alternatively, may over-emphasize culture. The consultee may fear being called a racist or unwittingly revealing prejudice. By allaying these fears by modeling ways to learn about the consultee's culture and discussing cultural issues objectively, rather than ignoring them, the consultant may help the consultee improve the consultee-client relationship.

In other situations, the consultant and the client may share the same culture with the consultee being from a different group. Here the consultee may view the consultant as an expert, and feel particularly vulnerable of making a cultural blunder. The consultant will need to maintain rapport by using one-downsmanship in areas not related to culture, by emphasizing commonality in other ways between the consultant and consultee, and tolerating but gently correcting cultural stereotypes. It may take an effort to maintain composure and keep the focus on the client in order to maintain a working partnership with the consultee (Ingraham, 2000).

Instances where the consultee and client share a culture, but the consultant is from a different group are less problematic. The consultant fosters rapport by demonstrating cultural sensitivity and by acknowledging the consultee's expert knowledge. On the other hand, the consultee may be uncomfortable with the cultural difference and fear criticism and bias on the part the consultant. The consultant will have to be patient, endure some testing, and work harder to demonstrate trust.

Three-way diversity is also a possibility when the consultant, consultee, and client are members of three different cultural groups. Ingraham observed, "Clearly, no one is the expert in three-way diversity. The consultant can use self-disclosure and one-downsmanship to identify the limits of his or her knowledge and skill with culture C, thereby reducing pressure on the consultee to have all the expertise. Through partnered learning, the consultant can establish a sense of 'we-ness' in learning about culture C, while modeling a process for cross-cultural learning and risk taking" (Ingraham, 2000, p. 336).

Maintaining the Relationship through Willingness Checks

Harris and Cancelli (1991) pointed out that there are differences in the extent to which consultees volunteer to participate in consultation. Some consultees are enthusiastic, some are willing, but some are resistant. Consultees who are coerced into consultation do not feel ownership of the process or the problem. "On the other hand, a consultee who consults under conditions of no pressure or reward (low justification) has greater pressure to develop a favorable evaluation of and commitment to consultation in order to avoid the cognitive dissonance of engaging in counter-attitudinal behavior" (Harris & Cancelli, 1991, p. 231). They suggest, among other techniques, that consultants continually emphasize the element of consultee choice. One way to do this is through willingness checks.

A willingness check is a question to the consultee inquiring as to their wish to continue the consultation discussion in the direction it is going or their intention to follow through on an action following the interview. In a simple form, the check might be, "Are we on the right track?" or "Is that something you are willing to do?" or "Does this make sense?" Questions such as these emphasize that the consultee has choices and is in control and the consultant is respectful of the consultee's participation.

Dealing with Reluctance and Resistance

Egan, in his textbook on counseling, offered advice on dealing with resistance (Egan, 2009). Many of his suggestions are similar to those described previously concerning building a nonhierarchical relationship built on mutual trust. Some of his additional thoughts were for the consultant to learn to see reluctance and resistance as normal in a helping relationship. The consultant should recognize that reluctance and resistance are sometimes a form of avoidance and are not necessarily due to ill will toward the consultant. He advocated for working directly with the consultee's reluctance and resistance rather than ignoring it, being intimidated by it, or being angry at the consultees for their behavior.

Guidelines for Building Relationships and Maintaining Rapport

Interpersonal-Behavioral

a) Obtain sanction from administrators to offer consultation.
b) Establish proximity by becoming a visible and trusted member of the staff of a school.
c) Decrease consultee's fear of the consultant and consultation.
d) Create an ethical contract with the consultee.
e) Engage in active listening to the consultee's presentation maintaining a nonjudgmental position.

f) Respond appropriately to feelings and emotions. Reduce consultee's anxieties and guilt about not being able to solve own problems by making statements that indicate understanding and acceptance of consultee's experience. Use body language and verbal reflection.

g) Maintain coordinate status through one-downsmanship and experience sharing.

h) Openly introduce and discuss issues of cultural diversity.

Intrapersonal-Cerebral

a) Assess administrator support and consultee expectations.
b) Determine consultee and administrator understanding of confidentiality.
c) Appraise the integrative capacities and ego strength of the consultee and the client.
d) Assess level of volunteerism.
e) Be aware of possible "testing."

Self-Monitoring Questions

a) How can I best define my role in this interaction with this individual?
b) How can I best be supportive and convey an understanding of this person's predicament without being condescending or relieving them of their responsibility for the problem?
c) Does the consultee feel comfortable sharing work-related problems with me?
d) Is the consultee trying to get me to take over the problem, seduce me into playing "psychotherapist," see if I am willing to "gossip" about others or maintain confidentiality, and so on?

References

Altrocchi, J. (1972). Mental health consultation. In S.E. Golann & C. Eisdorfer (Eds.), *Handbook of community mental health* (pp. 477–508). New York: Appleton-Century-Crofts.

Benjamin, A. (1969). *The helping interview.* Boston: Houghton Mifflin.

Brown, D., Pryzwansky, W.B., & Schulte, A.C. (2011). *Psychological consultation and collaboration.* Upper Saddle River, NJ: Pearson.

Caplan, G., & Caplan, R. B. (1993). *Mental health consultation and Collaboration.* San Francisco: Jossey-Bass.

Egan, G. (2009). *The skilled helper: A problem-management and opportunity-development approach to helping* (9th ed.). Belmont CA: Books/Cole, Cengage Learning.

Gibbs, J.T. (1980). The interpersonal orientation in mental health consultation: Toward a model of ethnic variations in consultation. *Journal of Community Psychology, 8,* 195–207.

Guvå, G. (2003). How to respond to teachers, who ask for help but not for consultation. In N.M. Lambert, I. Hylander, & J. Sandoval (Eds.), *Consultee-centered consultation: Improving the quality of professional services in schools and community organizations* (pp. 257–266). Mahwah, NJ: Lawrence Erlbaum.

Harris, A. H., & Cancelli, A. A. (1991). Teachers as volunteer consultees: Enthusiastic, willing or resistant participants? *Journal of Educational Psychological Consultation, 2,* 217–238.

Hughes, J.N. (1986). Ethnical issues in school consultation. *School Psychology Review, 15,* 489–499.

Ingraham, C.L. (2000). Consultation through a multicultural lens: Multicultural and cross-cultural consultation in schools. *School Psychology Review, 29,* 320–343.

Ingraham, C.L. (2003). Multicultural consultee-centered consultation: When novice consultants explore cultural hypotheses with experienced teacher consultees. *Journal of Educational & Psychological Consultation, 14,* 329–362.

Ingraham, C. (2004). Multicultural consultee-centered consultation: Supporting consultees in the development of cultural competence. In N.M. Lambert, I. Hylander, & J.H. Sandoval (Eds.), *Consultee-centered consultation: Improving the quality of professional services in schools and community organizations* (pp. 133–148). Mahwah, NJ: Lawrence Erlbaum Associates Publishers.

Ingraham, C.L., & Meyers, J. (Guest Eds.). (2000). Multicultural and cross-cultural consultation in schools: Cultural diversity issues in school consultation [Special issue]. *School Psychology Review, 29*(3).

Kelly, J.G. (1993). Gerald Caplan's paradigm: Bridging psychotherapy and public health practice. In W.P. Erchul (Ed.), *Consultation in community, school and organizational practice: Gerald Caplan's contributions to professional psychology* (pp. 75–85). New York: Taylor & Francis.

Sandoval, J., Lambert, N.M., & Davis, J.M. (1977). Consultation from the consultee's perspective. *Journal of School Psychology, 15,* 334–342.

Zins, J.E. (1981). Using data-based evaluation in developing school consultation services. In M.J. Curtis & J.E. Zins (Eds.), *The theory and practice of school consultation* (pp. 261–268). Springfield, IL: Charles C. Thomas.

4

PROBLEM EXPLORATION, DEFINITION, AND REFRAMING

A critical early step in the consultation process is problem identification, which overlaps the first stage of relationship building and maintaining rapport. The consultant is creating a rapport and engagement while listening to the consultee present their problem or problems. Novice consultants often wish to jump right into the problem-solving process and emerge with an instant solution, as do consultees. Consultants must recognize, however, that many times, the stated problem may be more complex than it first appears. Problem identification requires exploration that should not be unduly hurried.

One of the assumptions of consultee-centered consultation is that the consultee will have a basic idea of what the dilemma is about, although they may not wish to reveal it completely to the consultant. Some thoughts may be socially unacceptable or out of awareness and cannot be disclosed until the consultee feels safe and at ease.

Representations and Presentations

Hylander (2012) termed the initial conceptualization of a problem a *representation*. Other terms for the consultee's understanding might be schema or scenario. By listening to the consultee, the consultant, too, will form a representation or multiple representations of the problem. The consultee's articulation of their representation is called the *presentation*, which may or may not clearly reveal the underlying representation. Presentations are what consultees say and representations are what they think.

Initially the consultant's objective is to understand the consultee's representation of the problem. By prompting and facilitating the consultee's presentation and by asking questions, the consultant forms a clearer picture of the consultee's representation. The consultant is *approaching* the consultee's representation, to use another of Hylander's terms.

At the same time and based on the presentation and answers to questions, the consultant may be forming one or more different representations of the problem. The consultant's new representations may be close or far away from those of the consultee. If they are close, the consultee's difficulty might be related to lack of skill or lack of confidence. If there are multiple divergent representations between the consultant and consultee, it is more likely that consultation will need to bring about conceptual change on the part of the consultee, the consultant, or both. *Reframing* is another term for the process of inducing conceptual change.

The consultant must be open to shifting representations, including their own. First they identify the initial representation of the consultee, next they shift from the consultee's representation to their own representation, and finally, based new evidence collected during the course of consultation, they may shift again to yet another representation.

Representations have a cognitive component, an affective component, and a motivational component (Hylander, 2012). That is, the representation reflects what individuals think the problem is, how they feel about it, and what they are willing to do about it. Their thoughts, feelings, or willingness to act may not be acceptable and may cause their presentation to be too vague or too stereotyped. When this occurs, the consultant will never be able to identify the representation unless he or she can interact through asking questions and sharing thoughts in a calm, supportive, nonjudgmental fashion.

Because they have a motivational component, it is useful to have a representation of the problem that will lead to a change of behavior on the part of the consultee. It is important to note that the representation the consultee has when she or he enters consultation has not led to effective consultee action to this point. A better representation may be needed to move forward.

Using Questions in Problem Exploration and Reframing

Questions posed by the consultant to the consultee function as the vehicle for problem exploration, although other forms of data collection may be employed later. Caplan reflected, "My questioning never takes the form of a cross examination of the consultee. He does not feel that I am scrutinizing or testing his knowledge, actions, or attitudes. I accept and respect his current state of knowledge about the case. The purpose of my questions is to get as full a statement of this knowledge as possible, so that the two of us may try to understand the complications of the case and jointly wonder about possible patterns of forces and inner meanings in the client's life" (Caplan, 1970, p. 86). But questions also have the affect of demonstrating the consultant's expert knowledge and shedding light on a wider set of issues the consultee has not brought up (Caplan & Caplan, 1993). Thus, questions function to clarify and modify representations.

Types of Questions

Consultants skilled in counseling already have learned good practices in asking questions (Benjamin, 1978). A primary consultant skill involves asking open-ended questions. Open-ended questions require an elaborated response as opposed to closed questions (questions that can be answered with a yes or no or a single word) or double questions (questions that limit the consultee to two responses). Open-ended questions, along with responses such as reflection and restatement of the consultee's answer, allow the consultee to explore the problem more easily, and communicate that the consultant is listening carefully to what is being said. Hughes and DeForest (1993) demonstrated that consultees rated as less effective those consultants who used a high number of closed questions.

Questions can also be indirect as well as direct. Direct questions are straight inquires, yet it is evident that the consultant is asking a question and expecting a response. Often indirect questions are requests for further information or clarity. A classic example of an indirect question is, "tell me more about it." Repeating a portion of a consultee's statement in a questioning tone of voice also serves to explore ideas. For example, if the consultee says, "I feel foolish when he looks at me that way," a consultant may simply say "foolish?" stimulating an elaboration.

Another type of question is the inference question. An inference question is one that invites the consultee to share their thinking about the problem. A simple form is: "Why do you think she acts like that?" Hughes, Erchul, Yoon, Jackson, and Henington (1997) found that asking inference questions, although rare in their study, was associated with positive consultee evaluations of consultant effectiveness.

Avoiding Some of the Dangers in Using Questions

Consultants should avoid using the same format of open or indirect questions repeatedly or only open questions. Such over-usage results in stilted conversation, and the skilled consultant varies question formats. Consultants should also shun the temptation to ask questions to satisfy curiosity about irrelevant issues rather than to help the consultee explore. Asking too many questions in a short period can be perceived as grilling by the consultee.

"Why" questions need to be used carefully, since if asked about the consultee's actions, they may view the why as accusatory and judgmental rather than as a simple request for information. Why questions about the client's actions, on the other hand, may yield insight into the consultee's representation of the problem and are useful inference questions.

Consultants should also avoid asking rhetorical questions (i.e., questions to which they know the answer) as this practice communicates superiority. Caplan also observes, "I am careful to avoid questions that the consultee is likely not to be able to answer; where I am in doubt I phrase the questions in such a way that he does not lose face if he has not made the necessary observations" (Caplan & Caplan, 1993, p. 65).

Questions serve many functions. In helping explore the problem the consultant uses them to encourage the consultees to be more concrete when they are vague, and to guide the consultant in gaining a fuller understanding of the consultee's point of view. They illuminate what the client is like and how he or she is behaving. They also illuminate the consultee's representation of the problem and provide information about the source of consultee difficulty.

Focus of Exploration

Each of the parties in consultation may become the focus for problem exploration: the client, the consultee, and the consultant. The focus may shift back and forth, but the consultant must keep each of the perspectives in mind.

Focus on the Client

The problem is almost always explored with a focus on the client's behavior. The pioneering behavioral consultant Bergan (1977) developed interview protocols for exploring the problem based on the applied behavioral analysis of the client's behavior (See also Bergan & Kratochwill, 1990). The Bergan and Kratochwill book created a set of interviews containing examples of questions the consultant might pose to the consultee at various steps in the process. A consultant with grounding in applied behavioral analysis will find the guidance outlined in the Problem Identification Interview (PII) and the Problem Analysis Interview (PAI) very familiar and can focus on the client's behavior in a similar way.

The two interviews consist of sets of questions designed to identify explicit behaviors in the client that are causing problems for the consultee. First the consultant leads the consultee to specify behavioral objectives for the client based on the consultee's goals. Second the consultant and consultee select measures of client performance. Next the consultee and consultant collect and display baseline data, and finally they define the problem in terms of the discrepancy between observed performance and desired performance. If the client has not made progress toward the consultee's goals, consultation resumes with a further analysis of the problem. The consultant and consultee then closely examine the antecedent, consequent, and sequential conditions involved in the problem behavior. Subsequently they plan strategies based on learning theory to alter the client's behavior.

A more current approach to identifying the client's problem is the cognitive-behavioral model (Brown, Pryzwansky, & Schulte, 2011). This approach assumes that the client has a skill deficit and that it can be identified through functional behavioral assessment. Through questioning and observation the consultant hopes to determine antecedents, behaviors, and maintaining consequences of the behavior, as well as variations due to settings and contexts. In an interview, for example, the consultant might ask the consultee to specify a behavior in observable terms, provide examples, note the time, location, and context of the behavior, indicate the consultee's response to the behavior, and speculate on the function the behavior serves for the student.

Whether or not the consultant is a strict adherent to behavior theory, examining the details about the client's behavior and the circumstances is important. Questions about the client's family background, culture, values, interests, and abilities are also useful. The next chapter will discuss important individual differences that may have bearing on the client's contribution to the consultation problem and about which the consultant might inquire.

Focus on the Consultee

At the same time as inquiring about the client, consultants should keep in mind that the consultee's answers about the client are influenced by their worldview or prior theories and understandings of human behavior. They are responding with their perceptions of reality that another observer may view differently. For this reason, behaviorally oriented consultants focusing on the client often wish to collect information more directly (Witt, Gresham, & Noell, 1996) rather than use consultee reports, although they may have no choice initially. Nevertheless, understanding the consultee's conceptualization of the situation and the cognitive schemas the consultee is using will help in designing interventions that will have a better chance of being implemented and of being successful in restoring the relationship between the consultee and the client. Again, questions are the vehicle for exploring the consultee's view of the consultation dilemma, while exposing the relevant ideas of the consultee that will need to be addressed later in the consultation process.

Gunilla Guvå (2004) has suggested a number of specific questions to use to help identify the consultee's thinking. Table 4.1 lists some useful questions for a first interview.

Questions such as these are very helpful in illuminating the consultee's initial theory (or theories) of human behavior, in general, and the specific theory of what is causing the consultation predicament. Again, most of the consultant's questions are open-ended.

Another useful question to ask of all consultees is "What have you tried to address the problem?" This question has several virtues. It permits the consultant to understand how the consultee has translated her or his theory into action. Often action is revealing theories that are not explicitly stated. Of course this question also permits the consultant to avoid the trap of suggesting an action or strategy that has already been tried and has not been effective. This key question will be discussed again in the section on Sources of Difficulty and in Chapter 8 on generating interventions.

TABLE 4.1 Questions to assist the consultee present his or her story and reveal their representation of the problem (Guvå, 2004).

Focus and Intent	Examples
Focus on the client's problem	What is the problem with x? How old is x? What you mean is that x.
Focus on the history of the client and problem	When did it start? What were some critical past incidents? What had you heard about x before you met him?
Focus on the concrete here and now	Can you tell me when during the school day the client is at his worst? What did he do and how did others react?
Focus on the consultee's explanations	Why do you think this is so? Is there something that can help us understand the client? What do you think is going on?
Focus on the consultee's picture of the client	What does the client look like? Who does he/she remind you of?
Focus on the consultee's fantasies about the future	What do you think will happen if nothing is done?
Focus on other imaginations (ghosts) of importance	Have you met similar problems before?
Focus on the consultee's expectations of the consultant	What did you expect me to do for you when you asked for my assistance?

Attribution Errors

Attributions are hypotheses people make about why they and others behave the way they do (Pintrich & Schunk, 2002). Attributions may involve internal factors such as ability or external factors such as circumstances. In general, teachers tend to attribute pupils' academic and behavioral difficulties to factors external to the teacher, not to their own classroom practices (Hughes, 1992).

The consultant should be aware of several errors known to occur in individuals' explanations of the behavior of others. One bias, called the fundamental attribution error, is the tendency to overestimate the internal and underestimate the external factors when explaining the behaviors of others. Another is the self-serving bias, or the tendency to equate one's own successes to internal factors and failures to external attributes. If these errors are made, the consultee will likely represent the client's problem as resulting from aptitude, or effort (internal causes), rather than from health or task difficulty (external causes). To check on these biases, consultants may pose questions getting at both attributions, such as "What is it about the client's makeup/abilities/personality that seems to be causing this?" followed by "What might be going on in the client's world or environment that might be causing this?" By asking both questions, the consultant may open new possibilities.

Sources of Difficulty

The consultant will also be exploring possible sources of difficulty coming from the consultee. Table 2.1 contains signs associated with each of Caplan's sources of consultee difficulty. During problem exploration, the consultee may confess a lack of knowledge, skill, or confidence directly. The consultee might state, "I feel helpless in the face of this client's misbehavior." The consultant will need to follow-up to determine if the helplessness is a function of not knowing what to do, not knowing how to do it, or concerns about which course of action to take.

The question "What have you done previously with this or another client" provides insight into all three sources of difficulty. In the answer, consultees may reveal they have done nothing (lack of knowledge, skill, or confidence), have chosen an inappropriate intervention (lack of knowledge), or have implemented an appropriate intervention poorly (lack of skill or confidence).

Ideas about lack of objectivity may emerge from the consultee's representation when it is fully revealed. A discrepancy between the consultant's representation and the consultee's is one possible indicator that the consultee perceives the client subjectively. (Of course it might also indicate that the consultant is viewing the problem subjectively.) The presence of stereotypes about the consultee; strong emotion, either positive or negative; and exaggerated thoughts about possible outcomes for the client are other signs the consultee has lost a professional perspective. Detecting lack of objectivity is not an easy task. The consultant must listen carefully to what the consultee says and evaluate it against other data without challenging it, at least initially.

Addressing Cultural Issues

Many ideas that a consultee may have about a client may stem from the cultural background of the consultee, which may be different from that of the consultant or the client. In the consultee, these ideas may be stereotypes of the client (or the consultant). Ingraham (2000) pointed out that there are threats to consultee objectivity from filtering perceptions through stereotyping, from overemphasizing the role of culture, or from being insensitive to cultural norms and values operating in the consultation situation. She also described intervention paralysis, a threat to consultee self-confidence, where the consultee is aware of cultural differences but fearful of being inappropriate and considered a racist. Consultant responses to cultural issues include valuing and soliciting multiple perspectives, creating an emotionally safe environment where culture and race can be discussed, and supporting cross-cultural awareness and learning. Consultants must model comfort in asking questions about cultural issues and discussing possible explanations based on cultural norms, but must challenge cultural stereotypes when encountered.

Focus on the Consultant

The answers to questions permit the consultant to view the consultee's understanding of the problem and his or her underlying theories of behavior. However, the exploration process also provides the consultant with information to be used in forming his or her own tentative conceptualization of problem. The consultant's construction of the problem may be different from the consultee's or it may be similar.

In order to form a hypothesis about the problem, the consultants may need to ask additional questions to solicit information needed for their own conceptualization. Many of the questions posed in the behaviorally based PII may yield additional insights. But other theoretical perspectives may demand different kinds of questions. For example asking about what is known of the child's home circumstances and family constellation may provide information about external stresses and anxiety. Asking about peer relations and interests might reveal insights into the child's motivation. Asking about developmental milestones provides a picture of physical, emotional, or social capabilities.

In asking these questions to build the consultant's representation of the problem, the consultant is moving from Hylander's *approach* mode to the *free neutral* mode. That is, the consultant is asking questions to open up the possibilities of other formulations of the consultation problem. The questions should be in the spirit of brainstorming or free association with one question leading to another in a linear or possibly non-linear fashion. The attitude behind the question should be simple curiosity and there should be no implication that the consultee should have thought of asking him or herself the question first. The stance is neutral and nonjudgmental. In fact the consultee might also pose questions at this point, the answers to which might need to be pursued through further observation and data collection. Also part of the free-neutral mode are statements or observations on the part of the consultant.

Accessible Reasoning

Argyris and Schön (1996) have argued that in interpersonal problem solving, a key skill of the consultant, is making explicit to the consultee their own conceptualization of the problem drawn from the information that has emerged from the consultation interview. That is, the consultant makes his or her reasoning accessible to the consultee, and, more importantly, offers up his or her conceptualization for discussion and debate. By making the conceptualization explicit and putting it on the table, the consultee can correct any consultant misperceptions and offer supporting or conflicting information, thus sharing results in higher-quality joint constructions of representations of the problem (Brown et al., 2011).

When asking a question, a follow-up to the question can be an explanation of the thinking or reasoning behind the question. For example, a consultant might ask, "I wonder how the other children in the classroom react when Jimmy throws a tantrum? I ask, because it might be frightening or amusing to them, and that is the reaction Jimmy is looking for." Another formulation might be, "Sometimes children have not mastered the prerequisite skill to be successful at a task. Does Jimmy know his number facts?" In making the consultant's reasoning available to the client, the consultant is also able to demonstrate that he or she has several reasons for the client's behavior in mind. Some questions go to one possible explanation; other questions shed light on alternative possibilities the consultant is considering. Consultants demonstrate they are able to entertain multiple hypotheses. Monson and Frederickson (2002) demonstrated that consultants in training improve in their use of acceptable reasoning statements (and decline in their use of closed questions) and as a result, improve in their understanding of a teacher's problem situation.

Modeling accessible reasoning also influences consultees to do the same. The more the consultee is able to offer up alternative ideas about what the causes of the difficulty might be, the better. Encouraging the consultee to accept that there might be more than one explanation for a behavior and more than one solution, naturally leads to an experimental mind set. The consultant will be motivated to test the alternatives, reexamine past observations and assumptions, and possibly reframe the problem.

Consultant Leads in Consultation

Besides questions, the consultant may offer observations coming from a different point of view or perspective, with the aim of possibly defining the problem in an alternative way. These statements are called leads because they originate with the consultant and lead the consultee to a neutral consideration of possibilities. The consultant presents these statements tentatively, as food for thought, and often makes accessible the reasoning behind them. The consultee should understand that these leads are part of a brainstorming process and an attempt to find an alternative frame or frames for the problem. The consultant is not dismissing the consultee's representation, but rather simply proposing different ways of looking at the client's situation to expand problem space. The consultant also encourages the consultee to generate alternative explanations, by asking, for example, "can you think of other reasons for this destructive behavior?"

Leads also have the function of stimulating conceptual change. By noting anomalous data (i.e., pointing out where the consultee's representation does not work) and by highlighting dissonant evidence not predicted by the consultee's framework, the consultant helps build dissatisfaction with the current explanatory theory. The consultant may additionally comment on what is missing or unexplained in the consultee's statements of the problem, or note contradictions in what the consultee has said. Part of the conceptual change process is to confront anomalies and create a new way of framing the problem that explains more of the facts. Working in this way illustrates the consultant and consultee distancing themselves from the consultee's original representation of the problem. The consultant must be careful not to move the process in this direction too soon and must be prepared to move back to a more neutral stance in the face of resistance.

In addition to creating dissonance, the consultant may attempt to create a new way of framing the problem by reorganizing the information presented by the consultee. In reorganization the consultant uses the same facts or observations the consultee has generated, but fits them together differently to suggest an alternative explanation. The consultant may suggest a different cause for the observed effect, or offer an explanation for times when the client acts differently. Generally the consultant introduces new ideas from psychological theory to be discussed and verified. As the process proceeds, the consultant and consultee will likely decide whether or not the consultee's construction is adequate to explain this and other cases.

Dimensions of the Problem

From the consultation conversation, eventually, a problem will slowly be identified. The problem will be defined on a number of dimensions. First the problem will be defined in terms of what the client does and is not able to do. It is useful to specify the discrepancy between the current behavior and a desired future behavior, as this sets a goal for the consultation.

Second the problem is defined on the basis of possible explanations as to why the client behaves the way he or she does. If the consultee and consultant have settled on a single explanation, and are confident of it, they can begin planning an intervention. If they are not completely confident in the explanation, they can plan to collect additional data to verify their representation, always looking for disconfirmatory and anomalous data.

If the consultant and consultee have generated more than one explanation or multiple representations, that is, the initial representation has been reframed, the consultant and consultee can plan ways to test the validity of new conceptualizations through data collection. They begin to embark on an experimental process where more detective work is needed to learn more about the client. If the process has brought the consultant and consultee to a new theory about the client, the test will be to determine if the new theory explains more of the client's behavior and has applicability to other children.

The final dimension of the problem to be identified is the consultee's status in terms of the adequacy of their knowledge, skill, self-confidence, and objectivity. Chapter 2 contains a description of how the consultant might respond to each of these aspects of the problem. It is important to remember that these lacks in the consultee are not mutually exclusive. A consultee can, for example, lack both knowledge and objectivity at the same time.

In many cases, to address the consultee dimension of the problem there will be a need to obtain additional data about the client. The consultant and consultee can use data for reality testing, can learn about ways others have responded to similar client problems, and can gather information about local resources, as well as analyze the social system and context of the problem.

Setting Priorities

As the consultee continues to tell the story of the work problem, sometimes multiple problems come to light. If, after discussion, the multiple problem behaviors seem to stem from a similar cause and the consultee ends up with a single representation of the client's difficulty, the process can continue.

If the consultee describes multiple problems with multiple representations, it may be that the source of difficulty lies in the consultee. In any case, the consultant and consultee will need to engage in a process of setting priorities and choose which issue or client to tackle first. Attempting to address too many problems at once leads to confusion and distraction. The consultant must demonstrate a systematic approach to problem solving and confidence in the process.

It is often useful to work initially on what appears to be an easy problem. If the consultant is successful, it will establish trust and confidence in the consultee. The consultant acknowledges that some problems are easier to resolve than others, however, and does not let expectations get out of hand.

Guidelines for Building Relationships and Maintaining Rapport

Interpersonal-Behavioral

a) Listen the consultee's presentation of the problem with the goal of understanding the consultee's representation.
b) Use open-ended and indirect questions to explore consultee ideas and client behaviors.
c) Explore the client's behavior. Consider using a behavioral approach if the consultee seems willing. Inquire about possible external pressures on the child.
d) Explain reasons behind questions and statements as appropriate.
e) Continue to respond in ways to address the consultee's lack of knowledge, skill, confidence, or objectivity.

Intrapersonal-Cerebral

a) Formulate an appraisal of the consultee's understanding or theory of the consultee's problem (representation).
b) Evaluate consultee's lack of knowledge, skill, self-confidence, or objectivity.
c) Attend to consultee's attributions for client's behavior noting possible biases and errors.
d) Define the problem in terms of client behavior and best theories to explain behavior.
e) Evaluate appropriate mode, approach or free-neutral, to respond to the consultee.

Self-Monitoring Questions

a) Am I "grilling" the consultee with my questions?
b) Do the consultee's reactions seem "realistic" to me, or do they seem somewhat different from the way I am seeing things?
c) Are my thoughts about and feelings toward the consultee "realistic," or am I having thoughts and feelings not directly related to the consultation experience?
d) Does the consultee understand my thoughts and reasoning behind my questions and observations?
e) Am I still comfortable in discussing the consultation dilemma?
f) What are some theories I have about the causes of the consultation problem?

References

Argyris, C., & Schön, D.A. (1996) *Organizational learning II: Theory, method and practice.* Reading, MA: Addison-Wesley.

Benjamin, A. (1978). *The helping interview.* Boston: Houghton Mifflin.

Bergan, J.R. (1977). *Behavioral consultation.* New York: Merrill.

Bergan, J.R., & Kratochwill, T.R. (1990). *Behavioral consultation and therapy.* New York: Plenum.

Brown, D., Pryzwansky, W.B., & Schulte, A.C. (2011). *Psychological consultation and collaboration.* Upper Saddle River, NJ: Pearson.

Benjamin, A. (1969). *The helping interview.* Boston: Houghton Mifflin.

Caplan, G. (1963). Types of mental health consultation. *American Journal of Orthopsychiatry, 33,* 470–481.

Caplan, G. (1970). *The theory and practice of mental health consultation.* New York: Basic Books.

Caplan, G., & Caplan, R.B. (1993). *The theory and practice of mental health consultation.* San Francisco: Jossey Bass.

Caplan, G., Caplan, R.B., & Erchul, W.P. (1995). A contemporary view of mental health consultation: Comments on "Types of mental health consultation" by Gerald Caplan (1963). *Journal of Educational and Psychological Consultation, 6,* 23–30.

Guvå, G. (2004). How to respond to teachers, who ask for help but not for consultation. In N.M. Lambert, I. Hylander, & J. Sandoval (Eds.), *Consultee-centered consultation: Improving the quality of professional services in schools and community organizations* (pp. 257–266). Mahwah, NJ: Lawrence Erlbaum.

Hughes, J.N. (1992). Social psychology foundations of consultation. In F.J. Medway & T.P. Cafferty (Eds.), *School psychology: A social psychological perspective* (pp. 269–303). Hillsdale, NJ: Lawrence Erlbaum.

Hughes, J.N., & DeForest, P.A. (1993). Consultant directiveness and support as predictors of consultation outcomes. *Journal of School Psychology, 31,* 355–373.

Hughes, J.N., Erchul, W.P., Yoon, J., Jackson, T., & Henington, C. (1997). Consultant use of questions and its relationship to consultee evaluation of effectiveness. *Journal of School Psychology, 35,* 281–298.

Hylander, I. (2000). *Turning processes: The change of representations in consultee-centered case consultation.* Linköping, Sweden: Linköping Studies in Education and Psychology No. 74.

Hylander, I. (2012). Conceptual change through consultee-centered consultation: A theoretical model. *Consulting Psychology Journal: Practice And Research, 64,* 29–45.

Ingraham, C. L. (2000). Consultation through a multicultural lens: Multicultural and cross-cultural consultation in schools. *School Psychology Review, 29,* 320–343.

Kratochwill, T.R., & Bergan, J.R. (1990). *Behavioral consultation in applied settings: An individual guide.* New York: Plenum.

Monson, J.J., & Frederickson, N. (2002). Consultant problem understanding as a function of training in interviewing to promote accessible reasoning. *Journal of School Psychology, 40,* 197–212.

Pintrich, P.R., & Schunk, D.R. (2002). *Motivation in education* (2nd ed.). Upper Saddle River, NJ: Prentice Hall.

Posner, G.P., Strike, K.A., Hewson, P.W., & Gertzog, W.A. (1982). Accommodation of a scientific conception: Toward a theory of conceptual change. *Science Education, 66,* 211–227.

Witt, J.C., Gresham, F.M., & Noell, G.H. (1996). What's behavioral about behavioral consultation? *Journal of Educational and Psychological Consultation, 7,* 327–344.

5

GATHERING ADDITIONAL DATA ON THE CLIENT, THE CLIENT'S BACKGROUND, AND THE CLIENT'S COMMUNITY

At the point when the problem has been tentatively identified, it may become appropriate in the consultation process for the consultant and consultee to decide to collect additional information about the client or clients. New information to supplement what the consultee has already brought may add to the current representation of the client or modify the hypothesis about what is causing the problem. In many cases, however, additional information may not be necessary because the subjective evaluation of the consultant and consultee may be sufficient to plan interventions. After all, it is the consultee's subjective view of the world that is the most pertinent reality for the consultant and the client, not additional tests results or other objective measures of the client's situation.

When Collecting More Data or Information Is Useful

In classical Caplanian consultee-centered consultation, the only data used is what is gained from the interview with the consultee. However, Berlin (1977) took a different stance. He believed it was important for the consultee to engage in finding out more about the client and the client's background and the institutional setting before moving ahead with developing an intervention. Moreover, the consultant might participate in the process. "The consultant's offer to obtain some information from health facilities, etc., through the principal's office or direct phone calls enhances the collaboration" (Berlin, 1977, p. 37).

Using Caplan's (1970) scheme, when the problem is lack of confidence, it may be unnecessary to collect additional information about the client. It might be more useful for the consultee to learn how colleagues deal with similar matters than to learn more about the client.

When the problem appears to derive from lack of knowledge or lack of objectivity, and sometimes even from lack of skill on the consultee's part, it usually proves useful to supplement the evidence being considered. New data can help refine the representation of the client's problem and can assist in evaluating rival hypotheses.

Lack of knowledge may be of two sorts. The consultee may lack information about the psychology of clients in general; that is, about learning and developmental principles that apply in various situations. Additionally, the consultee may lack specific information about the individual client; that is, about the client's status with respect to educationally relevant individual differences. All consultants by virtue of their expertise are able to provide consultees with relevant general knowledge from their field. However, the consultant would handle the need for specific information differently, depending on consultee status. External- or community-based consultants do not usually collect information themselves on the client for use in the consultation dialogue. On the other hand, this data-gathering capacity and role on the part of the school-based consultant is a distinguishing feature of school-based consultation, and in many situations it is precisely this data-gathering attribute of the school-based consultant that leads to requests for consultation.

Whether counselor, nurse, school social worker, language specialist, or school psychologist, the school-based consultant has other nonconsultant roles in the school that also revolve around data collection. Because these activities are often more concrete and occupy more of the consultant's time than consultation, this data-gathering activity may be seen as the major, and perhaps exclusive, role of the consultant. School psychologists are supposed to test children (at least this is the most common perception of the profession on the part of teachers), and when testing is not going on, these specialists are somehow thought not to be doing their jobs. Because these expectations are so strongly held by certain consultees, *it is almost necessary* to establish the consultant's professional credibility for the consultant to engage in some direct services to the client, regardless of the kind of problem presented (Newman, 1967). Consultees who do not hold these same expectations for direct services from the consultant may be more tolerant when data collection does not occur.

The consultee is not the only one to hold expectations about assessment. Just as community-based consultants are warned to avoid slipping into the familiar mode of psychotherapy in their relationships with the consultee (Caplan, 1970), school-based consultants must be conscious of their own drives to move into a comfortable role in their relationships such as psychometrician or information interviewer. The consultant role is not an easy one, the outcomes are not as predictable as they are in other roles, and it is tempting to abandon the ambiguity of the consultation role for the security and clarity of working directly with the client. Assuming the role of consultant poses some risk of anxiety because of uncertainty. Solving human problems is hard; people have failed before the consultant is called in, and the consultant may feel accountable to deliver immediate answers. It is no wonder school-based consultants often flee to the safety of another role they know well, such as assessment or counseling.

When the collection of additional information would be helpful, data collection offers several opportunities to enrich the consultation process. Beyond establishing the professional credibility of the consultant, the act of offering to gather independent data demonstrates additional willingness to be involved in the problem and a commitment to work toward a solution. The consultant also acts as a model in his or her execution of the assessment process, exemplifying an experimental attitude and a data-based approach to decision making. Neutral reality testing can counter biases and unwarranted assumptions. Assessment is systematic and, to some extent, dispassionate. This resort to data collection is a forward move that allows suspension of anxiety about the problem because at least something is being done. This relief of anxiety alone may result in freeing the consultee from *over involvement* with the client so that a change in perception may take place.

There is a danger in the decision to collect more data. Many school people hold unrealistic expectations for the outcome of assessment. They believe that assessment devices have much more precision and much higher validity than is actually the case. They expect tests, for example, to pinpoint exact problems that children have in learning, and to yield information immediately translatable into classroom interventions. When this does not transpire, consultees are disappointed. Ironically, when the information produced turns out to yield few surprises and is more confirmatory than productive of new insights, teachers and administrators may feel that data collection was a waste of time. The consultant's task is to anticipate such unrealistic expectations for what may be forthcoming from information gathering, and be clear about what the purpose of the assessment is, how it will be done, what assessment can be expected to yield, and how valid that information is likely to be.

The Assessment Planning Conversation

One way these realistic expectations may be communicated to the consultee is through an assessment planning conversation. When it becomes clear that additional information about the client will be useful to the problem-solving process, there is a minor shift in the consultation relationship. The consultant contributes his or her expertise in data collection, assuming more leadership in the discussion. The focus turns to working out the objectives of the assessment, the possibilities, and who will be responsible. The consultant explains what domains of information might be assessed, what techniques might be used, and what limits there are on the accuracy and generalizability of the information to be collected. The consultant does not set out a smorgasbord of assessment devices from which the consultee chooses, but rather outlines what is possible, practical, and useful. The consultant is authoritative about assessment during this conference and works from the principle of the minimum valid assessment.

Minimum Valid Assessment

Briefly stated, the minimum valid assessment is the combination of the fewest domains and techniques of assessment that will yield sufficient information to continue the consultation problem-solving process. Collecting information is time consuming and invasive of privacy. Data should not be collected to satisfy simple curiosity but rather to address a hypothesis that has been generated during consultation.

Setting Responsibilities

Both the consultee and the consultant may have roles in collecting information. The consultee has more access to the setting than the consultant and can become a participant-observer. The information the consultee collects will have increased validity because it is collected in authentic contexts. At the same time, because the consultee has a teaching role in the classroom, it may be too distracting to observe carefully, or too difficult to make time to collect information from the client in one-on-one interactions. This is not to imply that the consultee cannot collect information but to acknowledge that the process will require extra effort.

In contrast, the consultant may have more time and freedom to collect information, but less access to the client. The consultant may only be at the client's school one day or a half-day per week. However the consultant may be able to approach sources of information, such as parents, physicians, or archival records, more easily than the consultee, and can do it from off-site. These differences in opportunity for data collection suggest that there might be a fruitful division of labor.

Since the collection of data will take time to plan, it will take place subsequent to the initial consultation session. At the initial session or anytime thereafter, the consultant and consultee can agree to do *mutual homework* prior to the next meeting. The consultee may agree to observe the child more closely during reading instruction and test the child's reading fluency while the consultant agrees to contact the district reading resource specialist and interview the parents about reading experiences at home. These mutual "homework" assignments are roughly equivalent in effort and both are designed to test hypotheses about the client's reading difficulties. However, often the consultee will need to spend more time collecting information because of access to the client and because of the need to do reality testing. The homework will be due at the next consultation session, which is set for when both parties will have additional information to share.

Sources of Information

Interviews

A common source of information or data about the client or setting is the informational interview. Informants who can provide additional insights about a student include other teachers who are currently working with the student, teachers or other personnel who know the student from the past, parents, peers, and community members. Either the consultee or the consultant may be able to contact these informants.

Observation

Much of the data collected by the consultee previously will have been observational. It is likely to be anecdotal rather than the result of systematic observation. During the assessment planning conference either the consultee or the consultant can decide to collect additional observational data to verify or challenge a hypothesis. Typically this observation will be structured rather than informal, and a number of resources are available to the teacher (and consultant) to learn observational techniques and strategies (e.g., Saginor, 2008; Wragg, 1999). Consultants with a background in behavioral assessment will have a reparatory of observational skills. A central activity in behavioral client-centered consultation is teaching consultees to collect observations, to collect baseline information, and to chart behavior change in the client (Martens & DiGennaro, 2008). These observations, particularly when data are graphed, serve as feedback to the consultee and promote treatment integrity (Noell, 2008).

Brown, Pryzwansky, and Schulte (2011) warned that for the consultee, when he or she feels unsure and overwhelmed, observation can be a cop-out serving to stall for time and no other purpose. Observation must have a clear rationale. If there is no purpose for the observation, and the consultant is simply taking a firsthand look, it suggests that the consultant distrusts the consultee's observation and wishes to see for him or herself. However, a consultee may invite observation if he or she lacks self-confidence or lacks knowledge and wishes to have a second set of eyes in the classroom for verification and validation.

Applied Behavioral Analysis

One approach to assessment most associated with behavioral consultation is applied behavioral analysis. During the problem identification phase discussed in the previous chapter, many times the consultant leads the consultee to define the problem in behavioral terms, possibly using a structured interview. Consultant questions lead the consultee to identify the behavior of most concern and then to operationalize it in observable terms and document the conditions under which it occurs. They discuss possible reinforcers for the behavior as well. The answers to the questions are usually from memory, however, and may not be accurate.

The consultant, typically in the data-gathering phase, will help the consultee devise a strategy, usually observational, to establish the frequency with which the behavior occurs in the natural setting. They will teach the strategy of behavioral observation and encourage the consultee to create a graph or other visualization of the data collected. This baseline information will later be used to evaluate the success of interventions, but first it will be used to determine the severity of the problem and set goals.

Archival Information

The school likely has a great deal of information archived about students, much of which is contained in a cumulative folder. Teachers often do not take the time to read this information or analyze it carefully. Information, which can shed light on a client's difficulties, includes previous test scores, grades, comments from previous teachers, health information, absences, disciplinary records, and demographic information. Various systems can be used to record and display this information, including graphs plotting growth or declines in performance over time. A key problem is getting teachers and other consultees to consider this as useful information from group standardized tests. Currently these tests have the reputation of being used to evaluate teachers and of having little relevance in informing instruction. Nevertheless, they may have something to contribute to thoughts about the client.

Another source of information is health and developmental history. School nurses or parents may be able to provide this information. Whatever the source, the consultant and consultee cannot overlook the possibility of biological contributors to the current consultation dilemma.

Portfolios

Portfolios are simply collections of student work (Jones, 2012). They may exist for a variety of purposes, including reporting and illustrating student achievement to parents, evaluating programs, or determining eligibility for special education. The portfolios may be collections of students' best work or may be aimed at typical work and teacher-made tests. Often assessors evaluate student work using rubrics, but another approach is to look for consistent errors pupils make in their work (e.g., Riccomini, 2005). Issues in the use of portfolios include the reliability and validity of the data produced and the time to collect and evaluate student products.

Formal and Informal Assessments

It is possible for either the consultee or consultant to assess the child directly in order to test hypotheses generated during the problem identification phase. Assessments can be based on standardized tests in formal assessment or on more informal tasks developed by teachers, such as curriculum-based measurement (Eckert, Codding, & Dunn, 2011) or curriculum-based assessment (Hintze, Christ, & Methe, 2006). In her form of consultee-centered consultation called

Instructional Consultation, Rosenfield stressed the use of data collection related to instructional practices and children's academic skill as a central part of the problem-solving practice (Rosenfield, 1987; Rosenfield, Silva, & Gravois, 2008).

Space does not permit a discussion of the multitude of formal assessment devices available to the consultant or consultee. It may be informative to discuss domains of individual differences that might be assessed to help determine more about the client's problem.

Individual Differences

In thinking and reading about educationally relevant individual differences, it is apparent that many of the same individual difference constructs are being viewed by researchers from different theoretical backgrounds, using different methodologies, from different subfields of study, using different sources of information and measures, and looking at different age groups. One can look at the concept of executive function, for example, from a cognitive developmental perspective, a psychometric perspective, a behavioral perspective, an information-processing perspective, and a neuropsychological perspective. Some investigators study infants and preschoolers, some school-age children, some college students, and some adults. Investigators use direct observation, self-report, test performance, and neural imaging, among other sources of information. As a result, different terms or labels may be used for the same phenomenon or individual characteristic. It is time to step back and identify a core set of individual differences.

Four domains emerge as important sources of individual differences relevant to both academic success and social-emotional adjustment. The two types of success are related. Academic success is key to emotional adjustment (especially in middle childhood), and emotional adjustment facilitates learning and thus academic success. In a sense, a predictor of one outcome will almost always correlate with the other. The four domains where constructs overlap are (a) Intellectual Capacity, (b) Personal Dispositions, (c) Engagement Dispositions or Motivation, and (d) Social Capacity. Constructs in these domains are influenced by a host of environmental factors (possibly starting prenatally) resulting in developed traits, talents, and attributes.

Figure 5.1 is a crude diagram of these four domains. The domains are represented by different shaded "clouds" within which are overlapping circles. The clouds are labeled with new, neutral descriptors for these domains. The circles within the domains are labeled with traditional areas of research on the psychology of individual differences. The overlaps in the circles and arrows represent possible overlaps in constructs. Toward the top of the diagram are more biologically determined constructs and domains. The bottom two domains develop later in childhood and are heavily influenced by constructs from the top domains as well as the environment.

The first domain is *Cognitive Capacity*. At least two sub-domains can be differentiated based on tradition. One is the research on Intelligence and another

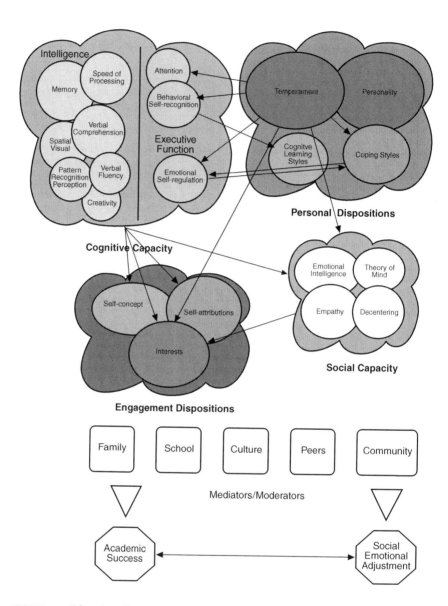

FIGURE 5.1 Educationally Relevant Individual Differences

is research on Executive Function. Although there are many notions about the components of *intelligence,* only some are listed. Note that creativity is a special case, in that it overlaps with some aspects of intelligence, but may have links to other constructs.

Having common characteristics with intelligence is *executive function,* represented in the right half of the domain Cognitive Capacity. Much of what is covered by the notion of executive function overlaps with intelligence, but it also contains the concepts of behavioral self-regulation, attention, and emotional self-regulation.

Executive function also has close links to the second domain, *Personal Dispositions.* The arrows indicate where overlap occurs. The dominant areas of research and theory in this domain are *temperament and personality.* These two sub-domains seem to overlap quite a bit. Some types of temperament are (1) adaptability/agreeable, (2) irritability/anger, (3) positive affect, (4) activity level, (5) persistence/effortful control, and (6) fearfulness. These temperament dimensions map fairly closely with the "big five" personality traits of (1) agreeableness, (2) extroversion, (3) emotional stability, (4) conscientiousness, and (5) openness. Related areas of research are cognitive and learning styles, which are related to executive function and behavioral self-regulation, as well as temperament. Much of the research on coping strategies indicates persistent individual differences related to emotion-centered coping and problem-centered coping, which also seem to be related to emotional and behavioral regulation.

The third domain, labeled *Engagement Dispositions,* represents constructs related to motivation. Ideas and beliefs about the self and interests result from both cognitive capacity and personal dispositions interacting with experiences from the environment. By middle childhood these individual differences begin to solidify and have an influence on academic and social-emotional outcomes. Of these areas, knowing about a child's interests as well as self-attributions provides useful information for intervention development.

The fourth domain is *Social Capacity.* There are several concepts related to the capacity to understand the world from another's point of view. Among them are concepts of *emotional intelligence, empathy, theory of mind, and egocentrism.* Developmental psychologists, neuropsychologists, and psychopathologists interested in autism, sociopathy, and violent behavior see social capacity as an underlying contributor to later social-emotional adjustment. Although the jury is still out on how much social capacity is biologically determined, it does appear to be an area of early individual differences. Emotional intelligence and social intelligence also have a research history and some of the components of these constructs are related to Cognitive Capacity as well as Social Capacity.

Clearly these early individual differences are moderated and mediated by the child's environment. Family, peers, school, culture, and community play an important part in shaping these individual differences. In planning interventions for the client it will be important to clarify and refine an understanding of his or her individual differences. Whether the individual differences are estimated from formal assessment or other sources, the consultant and consultee must consider what is unique about the client. Consultants can use Figure 5.1 as a reminder of the many ways clients differ.

Family and Cultural Background

Berlin (1967) observed that an important step in consultee-centered consultation is "an effort to increase the teacher's distance from the problem and his objectivity by using all the data provided to draw a picture of the etiology of a particular child's problems, showing how experience with important adults in the child's life have affected him and resulted in his present behavior" (p. 39). The consultant and consultee should explore the culture of the family and the community by inquiring into family history and dynamics. Information about the community in which the client dwells and peer relations outside of school can also provide insight into the origins of the problem. Much of this information will be collected through interviews with parents and cultural informants.

Guidelines for Gathering Additional Data

Interpersonal-Behavioral

a)   Decide whether more data will be needed or useful.
b)   Assign mutual homework.
c)   Assist consultee in learning about behavioral or other observation systems.
d)   Collect data on clients as appropriate to professional role.

Intrapersonal-Cerebral

a)   Determine what data is appropriate to collect, and from what sources.
b)   Consider how culture, family, and community might impact the client or consultee.
c)   Determine what data will address consultee's lacks.

Self-Monitoring Questions

a)   Will more information address the consultee's needs?
b)   What data will help in evaluating hypotheses we have generated?
c)   Have we collected only the data necessary and avoided invading privacy?
d)   Which sources of information should be tapped?
e)   What do we know or what could we learn about the client's individual make up in the four domains of Cognitive Capacity, Personal Dispositions, Engagement Dispositions, and Social Capacity?

References

Berlin, I. N. (1967). Preventive aspects of mental health consultation to schools. *Mental Hygiene, 51*, 34–40.

Berlin, I.N. (1977). Some lessons learned in 25 years of mental health consultation to schools. In S.C. Plog & P.I. Ahmed (Eds.), *Principles and techniques of mental health consultation* (pp. 23–48). New York: Plenum Publishing Corporation.

Brown, D., Pryzwansky, W.B., & Schulte, A.C. (2011). *Psychological consultation and collaboration*. Upper Saddle River, NJ: Pearson.

Caplan, G. (1970). *The theory and practice of mental health consultation*. New York: Basic Books.

Eckert, T.L., Codding, R.S., & Dunn, E.K. (2011). Curriculum-based measurement. In A.S. Davis (Ed.), *Handbook of pediatric neuropsychology* (pp. 1137–1143). New York: Springer.

Hintze, J.M., Christ, T.J., & Methe, S.A. (2006). Curriculum based assessment. *Psychology in the Schools, 43*, 45–56.

Jones, J. (2012). Portfolios as "learning companions" for children and a means to support and assess language learning in the primary school. *Education, 40*, 401–416.

Martens, B.K., & DiGennaro, F.D. (2008). Behavioral consultation. In W.P. Erchul & S.M. Sheridan (Eds.), *Handbook of research in school consultation* (pp. 147–170). New York: Erlbaum/ Taylor & Francis.

Newman, R.G. (1967). *Psychological consultation in the schools: A catalyst for learning*. Oxford, England: Basic Books.

Noell, G.H. (2008). Research examining the relationships among consultation process, treatment integrity, and outcomes. In W.P. Erchul & S.M. Sheridan (Eds.), *Handbook of research in school consultation* (pp. 323–341). New York: Erlbaum/ Taylor & Francis.

Riccomini, P.J. (2005). Identification and remediation of systematic error patterns in subtraction. *Learning Disabilities Quarterly, 28*, 233–242.

Rosenfield, S.A. (1987). *Instructional Consultation*. Hillsdale, NJ: Lawrence Erlbaum.

Rosenfield, S.A., Silva, A., & Gravois, T.A. (2008). Bringing instructional consultation to scale. In W.P. Erchul & S.M. Sheridan (Eds.), *Handbook of research in school consultation* (pp. 203–223). New York: Erlbaum/ Taylor & Francis.

Saginor, N. (2008). *Diagnostic classroom observation: Moving beyond best practice*. Thousand Oaks, CA: Corwin Press.

Wragg, E.C. (1999). *An introduction to classroom observation (2nd ed.)*. London: Routledge.

6
SHARING INFORMATION, HYPOTHESIS GENERATION, AND REFRAMING

There are at least two points during consultation when data may be collected and shared. First, early in consultation the consultee and consultant may wish for additional information to clarify or confirm the consultation problem. The second occasion occurs after consultees have implemented an intervention or initiated a change in their own behavior. The consultant and consultee use the second set of data to evaluate whether the intervention was implemented correctly and has resulted in improvement in the client. This chapter will focus primarily on the first sort of data collection, although many of the issues will be relevant to the second. The second use of data will be discussed in Chapter 10.

Once the consultant and the consultee have agreed to collect data to understand the needs or circumstances of the consultee, they will need to schedule a session to discuss the results. In this session, both the consultant and the consultee will be presenting information and the following general principles may guide the conversation. In giving information, it is important to:

Be wary of assuming the authority position.
Present the information clearly.
Evaluate the accuracy of the information.
Invite the other to react to the information.
Get feedback from the consultee.
Allow for and encourage assimilation of the information.

Most mental health professionals working in the school already have a data-collection role. School psychologists and counselors often work with test results and social workers typically report information gained from interviews and from archival records. They are used to present information and have developed their own styles and techniques for sharing results. Since it is an essential part of their role, and they perform it routinely, there is a slight danger that they will be perceived as being in an authority position, disrupting the nonhierarchical nature of consultee-centered consultation. At the same time, the consultant will be modeling how to present information and communicating important attitudes about how to interpret data.

Avoiding the Authority Position

One of the first principles of data sharing is not to overwhelm the consultee with too much data at once. Since school-based consultants are used to present data, they may have had time to collect quite a bit, and they may wish to share it all. They may have an impressive amount to share, but supplying substantially more than the consultee has been able to collect elevates their expert status. In addition, giving too much information at once makes it difficult for the listener to process and absorb the implications.

As a result the consultant must be prepared to use one-downsmanship statements during the data-sharing conversation. For example, the consultant can acknowledge that their information is generated by hearsay or in artificial settings, whereas the teacher is able to see behavior in a natural and highly relevant context. Remembering to be modest and acknowledging the other's expertise is important. At the same time it is possible for the consultant to own his or her special expertise. The consultant likely has time and skills to obtain useful information about the client in other contexts and circumstances.

As in other phases of consultation it is important to share the reasoning underlying any interpretations or conclusions drawn from data. By explaining his or her thinking, the consultant is demonstrating an openness to discussion and modeling different ways to think about the client.

Be self-critical. The consultant should be objective about the difficulties he or she has in collecting the information. The consultant wishes to communicate that he or she is sympathetic to the problems the consultee may have collecting data.

Making Sure the Information Is Presented Clearly

One of the better ways to increase comprehension is to present data visually. Not all information can be presented this way, but behaviors lend themselves to being graphed and charted. Particularly if baseline information is available, dramatic changes are often evident following an intervention. Even if baseline has not been taken, behavioral frequency can be plotted against time or day or subject matter taught or otherwise correlated with events that occur in the classroom. Does, for example, disruptive behavior and talking out decrease during music instruction and then increase during social studies? Seeing it visually portrayed may help the consultant and consultee consider different aspects of intervention.

Normative data from standardized tests is usually reported in percentiles or standard scores. A chart of the normal curve plotting both standard scores and percentiles often brings home the message of how unusual or how common the score is with reference to peers.

Although not yet common in schools, increasingly it is feasible and inexpensive to record behavior on digital cameras. Recording the client in natural settings and playing back a video during consultation may be useful in examining a number of subtle aspects of the problem behavior that cannot be done in real time. It is, of course, difficult to be sure that a camera is focused on the right place at the right time, and it is time consuming to review and isolate particular scenes, but the effort may be worthwhile. A carefully selected and edited sequence may produce a number of insights.

Because memory is fallible, having written documentation to refer to is also useful. Interview notes or even transcripts of recordings could be shared and jointly examined. Exact quotations will assure that the information from sources not present will be accurately understood.

Delivering information clearly involves planning to organize both the information and presentation. The consultant must give thought to the issue of confidentiality; that is what information may be shared and how it will be protected from those not involved in the consultation process. In presenting information, typically the consultant presents positive information about strengths and competencies first. Since there is a tendency to be negative about the client and to focus on deficits of one kind or another, examining the positive allows the consultant to challenge stereotypic thinking. As will be discussed later, in order to avoid cognitive biases, the consultant and consultee should spend equal time using data to confirm and disconfirm representations they have of the problem.

One thing that cannot be planned in advance of presenting the data is the pace at which it will be presented. Of course the consultant will not want to bombard or overwhelm the consultee with information. Going through things too slowly is also not helpful if the consultee is ready to move ahead. Finding the right balanced pace is part of the art of consultation.

Involving the Consultee

The consultee cannot be a passive recipient of information. One strategy to begin the conversation is to ask consultees for their prediction of the results of the assessment before hearing them: "What do you think I was able to learn or observe?" or "How do you think the assessment turned out?" The consultee's response will indicate their expectations and give insight into presentations and representations. They will likely have information to share, but in addition the consultant can check whether or not the information presented has been understood via a comprehension check. A usual criterion is to determine if the consultee can rephrase in their own words what has been said to them. Without being condescending, the consultant might ask: "How would you describe what we have found?" or "What could we say to others that we have learned?" The consultant should also check to see how the consultee reacts to the information. The consultant might ask: "Do these results make sense to you?" or "Do you understand how these data were obtained and what do you think they may mean?"

More importantly the consultant should ask for confirmatory and disconfirmatory information by asking such questions as:

> Has the consultee seen similar behavior?
> Does this make sense in terms of other information?
> Has the consultee found exceptions?

In general, the presentation of data should be followed by inquiries into new thoughts and ideas that may emerge. Has the presentation or representation changed? The information collected may create dissonance in the consultee and he or she should have a chance to process it. More on this point will be covered later.

Receiving Information from the Consultee

The consultant may also be receiving new data and insights from the consultee, and must ask him or herself the same questions. First the consultant determines what data the consultee has been able to collect assuming mutual homework was agreed upon. Then the consultant should be able to summarize what he or she has heard. Again the consultant may comment after the information has been presented on how it agrees or disagrees with information he or she has collected.

The consultee may have not collected any information in spite of agreeing to do so, or may have only made a minimal effort. The consultant will need to determine the reason for this failure in a nonjudgmental manner, since there may be an unanticipated problem. This failure may also be a sign of resistance on the part of the consultee and should be addressed. Whatever the reason, if it can be overcome, the consultee should be encouraged to fulfill a commitment. The consultant can be patient and encourage future data collection.

Encouraging Assimilation and Accommodation

Absorbing new information takes time if deep processing is to occur. Those getting new information need to consider how it fits with what they already know or change their understandings to accommodate the new data. If the topic shifts too quickly there may not be time for this reflection to occur. In addition the consultant may encourage reflection by asking: "How does this new information fit or not fit with what we already know (our representations)?" Give the consultee time to absorb the information.

Discuss Accuracy

It is good practice to take time to evaluate the accuracy of the information being examined. All information should be questioned as to its reliability and its validity. Often information is collected at one point in time. In this case, the questions to ask are "Will the findings be the same on another occasion?"; "Will the findings apply to other settings?"; "How valid is the information?"; "Is it really a reflection of the underlying phenomenon we are interested in?" or "Is there a need to validate this information?"

One approach to evaluating information is through an examination of convergent and divergent validity (Campbell & Fiske, 1959). Data are deemed valid when information from multiple sources and multiple methods of data collection agrees. This agreement suggests measurement accuracy. However, in some cases it is useful to know that the information obtained from one source or context does not agree. For example, if we suspect a child's inattention is not due to biological factors, we feel more confident in this hypothesis when he is inattentive in the classroom but not in other settings or with other people who make similar demands for sustained attention. Anomalous data stimulate reframing.

One conclusion from this discussion might be that the data collected are not accurate or sufficient to proceed to intervention, and there is a need for more or different information. This may be a disappointing outcome, but can serve as a lesson that human problems are not easy to solve, and if they were, consultation would not be necessary. Also this outcome should not be viewed as unusual. Assessment is often a stochastic process with the answer to one question leading to a new question. Instead the consultant should be prepared to return to an early phase and plan more data collection with the consultee's collaboration.

A Caution about Convergent Information—Cognitive Bias

There are a number of biases in human cognition that lead to poor decision making (Gambrill, 2012). Perhaps the most pernicious of these biases is the need to confirm expectations or to verify preconceptions. This is termed the *confirmatory* bias. Most of us have a tendency to selectively attend to information compatible with our already established theory of how the world works. Many clinicians use a parallel tendency in their clients when they use projective methods. These techniques are predicated on the notion that a person's attitudes and cognitions about how the world operates will be displayed when the client is confronted with ambiguous stimuli. In clinical interviews, this bias manifests itself as transference; the patient brings attitudes previously formed about significant others and assigns them to the therapist. Clinicians, aware that this bias is universal, guard against countertransference, fearing that their own predispositions or unconscious motives will lead them to attend to only some aspects of a case. A cognitive explanation for the confirmatory bias is the resistance to change of schemas or representations, once established. When a conceptualization is established, new information is assimilated into what is already understood; only rarely does accommodation take place with its concomitant conceptual change (Sandoval, 1996). Cultural and other stereotypes are examples of schemas that may influence how information is collected or interpreted. Not only do we act to confirm hypotheses, we also do not readily accept or appreciate that things can occur by chance—we want them to occur for a reason. As a result we are prone to attribute behavior or events to causes, and come up with explanations for chance variation.

Another bias operating when we collect or interpret information is the *availability* bias. Errors occur when we are influenced by vivid information and information similar to recently experienced events. We recall this available information more easily. Again, schema theory provides an explanation. If a schema is activated or brought to mind by lively, fresh, and extreme information, that schema will be more easily reactivated in the immediate future because of strengthened links between short- and long-term memory. We all have experienced learning a new word or fact for the first time and then subsequently encountering it again and again. A variation on the availability bias is the *anchoring heuristic*. This is the tendency to rely more heavily on information received early in the process of gathering information than on data received later. The first encountered information, because it is more available in memory, acts as an anchor to influence subsequent perception and memory.

An allied phenomenon, related to the availability and confirmatory bias, is the *halo* effect. This is the tendency to be unduly influenced by a single positive or negative trait on the evaluation of other, unrelated traits or behaviors. A common example is when the attractive appearance of an individual leads to unearned positive evaluations of competence in academic performance.

The best way to guard against these biases is to place an even-handed focus on convergent and divergent information. This means actively seeing information that is inconsistent with a consultee's or consultant's representations of the problem, as well as information that supports it. Best practice is to seek information from multiple data sources and compare it, recognizing that different sources will have different strengths and weaknesses and seeing the child in different contexts. Just as we hope to find convergence between sources, it is also important to attend to divergences. Discrepancies in information can come from different demands in different settings, differences in motivation, differences in measurement techniques, and differences in the knowledge or values of the informants. Discrepancies can also open the door to new ideas and new ways of thinking about the client.

Electronic Data Sharing in Consultation

One question that might arise is does the information need to be shared in person. Can data be discussed and examined using e-mail, videoconferencing, or other means? Current technology and pressures on time and resources suggest that these tools might be integrated into consultation. E-mail, for example, has the advantage of being quick and available to be read when convenient. However, misunderstandings do occur, and it takes a great deal of time to clear them up. Videoconferencing or other forms of synchronous communication make possible more back and forth discussion and are an improvement. However, important nonverbal nuances are often lost at a distance, and the camera is not always flexible enough to capture subtlety. In addition, there are concerns about confidentiality, as third parties can "hack" into communications, either purposely or inadvertently. Nevertheless electronic tools will no doubt be used in consultation in the future.

Hypothesis Generation and Reframing

The consultee and consultant have sought additional information to clarify existing representations of the problem or to construct a new one that will be used as the basis for treatment planning. The data will also help accept or reject competing hypothetical explanations. If the data support one representation over another, the way forward may be clearer.

If there is to be a change in a representation, the participants must become dissatisfied with their old way of thinking about the problem. This dissatisfaction will come from data not predicted by their original conceptualization, new information to assimilate, or data disconfirming a basic assumption. Thinking the client has below average academic ability, the consultant or consultee may discover that there has been a recent death in the client's family, for example, or that the client has scored in the superior range on an achievement test.

The most likely impetus for changing our representation of the problem comes from contradictory information that has been discovered and verified; information that must be explained. The consultant and consultee must resist the temptation when faced with contradictions to resolve them quickly by discounting some of the information as invalid or ignoring them. Instead, at least initially, they should seek to reframe the client problem (and possibly the consultee's lack of objectivity) by creating a new formulation that allows the contradictory or anomalous information to make sense. Since the previous representation of the problem has probably not been working, there should be extra incentive to think about the client differently. The consultant may ask, "How can we reconcile what we have learned at this point?" or "Does it make sense that we have learned this on the one hand and that on the other?"

Reframing is a creative process. To reframe, the consultant and consultee must step back from their past ideas and consider the assumptions, beliefs, and theories they have used to create this representation. Then they must consider another way of assembling the facts at hand. To start they can challenge their assumptions. They may shift the direction of cause and effect, or look for other, previously ignored factors or variables that may be contributing to the problem. They may expand the frame from dynamics in the classroom to influences from the culture of the school or the community. Another strategy is to examine and question conventional wisdom.

If the consultant has helped the consultee manage emotion and created a neutral "playground" where the consultant and consultee are able to consider ideas on their own merit and reject or accept them on the basis of the preponderance of evidence, the consultant should be free to introduce their own representations as possible new frames for the problem. The consultant is free to make his or her reasoning accessible. In Hylander's (2012) terms, the consultant begins to move the consultation away from the consultee's initial representation, while oscillating between confirming and challenging the consultee's presentation and their own representation.

Creating a New Working Hypothesis

The outcome of reframing should be a new working hypothesis, or mutual representation of the consultation problem. It is mutual in the sense that it has been derived by both parties and is acceptable to both the consultee and consultant. The consultant may hold alternative representations about the consultee's contribution or about the client, but accepts that the new representation or hypothesis is viable and plausible to the consultee. The new hypothesis should have the virtue of restoring some optimism to the consultee and offering new ideas for action.

Draw Inferences for Intervention

Another rationale for collecting data is to suggest interventions. Observations of the client may lead fairly directly to behavioral intervention, particularly if obvious contingencies and reinforcers are noted during the observation. If the consultee and consultant have identified certain antecedents and consequences of undesired behaviors, these may become the targets for change.

To take another example, if observations and interviews have verified that the child is insolent, refuses to do work, and is aggressive; have verified that correction is not effective; and have verified that the consultee's classroom leadership is constantly challenged, the consultant and consultee might turn to an Adlerian perspective (Dreikurs & Grey, 1968). The representation will become that the child has a goal to gain power (as opposed to gain attention, seek revenge, or display inadequacy). The intervention that will follow will be to help the child understand his goal, avoid power struggles with the child, find opportunities for cooperation, and make the child feel important in the classroom. The collection and sharing of information is to create or fine-tune representations and hypothesis that can be tested through a trial intervention. Chapter 8 will discuss the generation of interventions such as this theory based strategy in more detail. First, however, it is important to consider the social context in which consultation takes place that might constrain consultation, the consultee, and the feasibility of intervention.

Guidelines for Sharing Information and Hypothesis Generation

Interpersonal-Behavioral

a)   Present the information clearly.
b)   Evaluate the accuracy of the information.
c)   Invite the consultee to react to the information.
d)   Get feedback from the consultee about the understanding and interpretation of new information.
e)   Allow for and encourage assimilation of the information.
f)   Point out contradictions and anomalies in the data.
g)   Establish a working hypothesis or hypotheses.
h)   Draw inferences for intervention.

Intrapersonal-Cerebral

a)   Be wary of assuming the authority position.
b)   Assess consultee understanding.
c)   Determine the extent to which the consultee is willing to collect data.
d)   Consider possible cognitive biases that may be operating in interpreting new information.
e)   Evaluate possible new representations of the problem the consultee may have.
f)   Assess whether the conditions for conceptual change exist.
g)   Evaluate the need to change own conceptualization or representation.

Self-Monitoring Questions

a)   Have I organized my information clearly?
b)   Have I made my reasoning accessible?
c)   Do I understand what the consultee has presented?
d)   Am I challenging the consultee with too much information?
e)   Am I able to reframe the problem based on new information?
f)   Do I have some tentative ideas for intervention?
g)   Have I been appropriately attentive?

References

Campbell, D.T., & Fiske, D.W. (1959). Convergent and discriminant validation by the multitrait-multimethod matrix. *Psychological Bulletin, 56*, 81–105.

Dreikurs, R., & Grey, L. (1968). *Logical consequences: A new approach to discipline.* New York: Meredith Press.

Gambrill, E.D. (2012). *Critical thinking in clinical practice: Improving the quality of judgment and decisions* (3rd ed.). Hoboken, NJ: John Wiley.

Hylander, I. (2012). Conceptual change through consultee-centered consultation: A theoretical model. *Consulting Psychology Journal: Practice and Research, 64*, 29–45.

Sandoval, J. (1996). Constructivism, consultee-centered consultation, and conceptual change. *Journal of Educational & Psychological Consultation, 7*, 89–97.

7

ANALYZING SYSTEMIC FORCES

The Social Context of the Schools

> Psychiatric consultation with several school systems has convinced me that most problem teachers become so as the result of certain pressures and practices that seem inherent in many school systems. I rarely have seen a teacher in consultation whose difficulties resulted only from her own personality problems. (Berlin, 1960, p. 827)

Because of the mental-health origin of consultee-centered consultation, the reader might conclude that consultants take the position that teachers and administrators need consultation because they are ignorant, ill prepared for their jobs, or have personal conflicts that interfere with their professional functioning with children. Indeed, both in the first two chapters and elsewhere, Caplan's taxonomy of consultee-based reasons for work difficulty appears. However, it is not at all accurate to imply that all work difficulties spring from consultee deficits in knowledge, objectivity, and so on; consultees have other reasons for not reaching their full professional potential. Although many professional difficulties do fit neatly into Caplan's scheme, and these are often more readily solvable than environmentally or institutionally induced difficulties, it is essential to recognize that many difficulties arise because of forces over which the consultee has little control. Consultees are aware of this fact and tend to ascribe many of their difficulties as educators to these environmental forces. Part of the school-based consultant's task, then, is to help the consultee examine the social factors acting in a particular problem situation and to help the consultee isolate what *can* be done and what *is* possible, given the sometimes overwhelming conditions producing a problem. For this reason, previous chapters have advocated that consultants shift focus during consultation to frame the problem in multiple ways.

A method has been developed for consultants to attack directly some of the social and organizational problems that interfere with the effective delivery of educational services to children. Using organizational development theory and technique (Schmuck & Runkle, 1984; Gallessich, 1982), an organizational consultant, working with those in positions of power and influence in an organization, can help the organization reevaluate traditional roles and procedures in the service of creating more effective ways to achieve their institutional objectives. It is the rare school-based consultant who can negotiate such a role or be effective if such a role is negotiated, because of problems of credibility and objectivity. An expert from outside the school is usually more effective in getting a system to examine itself. Nevertheless, readers may wish to familiarize themselves with organizational development approaches to consultation, particularly if they are external to the school system.

Consultee-centered consultants working within the system cannot ignore the organizational or ecological context of the consultation problem, particularly when beginning to plan interventions that must be workable in a particular setting. What are some of the social and environmental forces at work in the school that are acting on teachers, administrators, and other school personnel making certain actions or changes possible and easy and others impossible or difficult? How does the school as a system create barriers to change and interfere with the stated objective of the school? In a brilliant classical book, Seymour Sarason (1996) has begun the task of describing some of the special constraints acting on school people that inhibit them from considering all of the alternatives for action open to them. *The Culture of the School and the Problem of Change* is a volume that all school-based consultants should read and reread as they attempt to establish consultative relationships. As the consultant and consultee begin to plan interventions, it is important to consider features of the system that may facilitate or impede a change.

The Teacher's Position in the School System

The phrase "school system" has been in use for a long time. With the advent of systems theory and social psychology, the term has taken on new meaning. If the classroom and the school can be thought of as a system, the teacher is obviously the central feature of the organization. As members of the system, teachers view their job as being responsible for the learning of skills, the acquisition of knowledge, and the creation of attitudes and predispositions toward learning on the part of their charges. The number of children for whom they are responsible varies from five or six in some special education classes to 30 or 35 in many elementary grade classrooms and up to 150 or more in secondary education classrooms. Of course, high school and junior high school teachers deal with only 30 to 35 at one time.

In addition, a curriculum has been established to help the teacher transmit knowledge, and a timetable has been set out for the accomplishment of the task. In the rare event that a curriculum has not been set by others, the teachers must create their own. A teacher's feeling of accomplishment is based on the notion that at the end of the year all or the majority of the children will have reached some minimum proficiency, usually a year's academic growth. As Sarason points out, "Faced with numbers and diversity of children *and* the pressure to adhere to a time schedule presents the teacher not with a difficult task but an impossible one" (Sarason, 1971, p. 152).

It takes a while for teachers to come to realize that their expectations for their class are unrealistic, if they ever do. Many believe that with a superhuman effort and with certain conditions satisfied, they would be able to come close to their goal. If one were to ask teachers what stands in the way of successfully meeting their objectives, as we have done, most would produce a list somewhat like the following section titles.

The Number of Children is Too Large

There is a great deal of literature on the class size debate. Not only would it not be financially feasible to reduce class size substantially, but there is not a great deal of research evidence showing significant improvement in pupil achievement with reduced class size until one reaches the size of 12 to 15 pupils. Nevertheless, from the teacher's point of view, which is the reality with which the consultant must be concerned, 30 children are a lot of individuals to manage at one time. With a group such as a classroom, with one acknowledged group leader (the teacher) and other informal leaders (the students), the group's dynamics are complex (see for instance Schmuck & Schmuck, 2000). Often without the teacher realizing it, the atmosphere of the classroom may become established around work and play goals set by students, and a variety of classroom subgroups will form among the children. Group norms for behavior have been inculcated in the students' former classrooms, at home, and in the neighborhood, and are transported into a new classroom often without the teacher's conscious realization of the process. The classroom is a microcosm in which the children get assigned various roles. Cliques form, scapegoating may begin, and competition can grow out of hand. Once social patterns have been established, they can be extremely difficult to alter, particularly if the group has been together prior to coming into the current teacher's classroom.

In large classes the teacher who wishes to move toward more individualized instruction has even more difficulty. There will be more diversity and individual lesson plans to prepare. In addition, a large amount of the teacher's day will be taken up with monitoring, evaluating, and helping the children achieve their individual objectives.

Another problem stemming from class size is the pure physical effort required to deal with a large number of people. The teacher must be "on stage" for long periods of time attending to children's requests, monitoring the progress of children, and meting out discipline. All of this activity may be accompanied with a constant barrage of noise. This is not to imply that noise, per se, is bad; rather, it is often the sign of an active, engaged classroom. Nevertheless, the physical demand of attending under these circumstances is extremely fatiguing. For the elementary grade teacher in particular, there are very few opportunities to be alone for a few quiet moments during the day to rest and recuperate. Industrial safety boards in most private enterprises would not tolerate the conditions of noise and distractions under which many teachers must function. Urban schoolteacher is usually listed as the most stressful occupation, ahead of air traffic controller, in modern America.

The consultant must remember that the demands on teachers to cope with large numbers of children are real. It is difficult to find extra time to give to a particular child or even to arrange to meet with the consultant. Levine (1972) reminds us, "The fact that we have to struggle to find the time and place to be consultants is important to note. That fact tells us that what is important to us is not necessarily important to others, and that workers in settings unfamiliar to us may perceive other tasks as critical for them" (pp. 9–10). Although it is not easy, methods for individualizing instruction can result in the teacher having more contact time with individual children, and the social climate of the classroom can be developed so that group dynamics will work to support teachers in their role. Teachers may transcend the numbers problem, but it is a genuine obstacle to effective teaching and the introduction of a new intervention in the classroom.

Children's Home Environments Do Not Support Them Sufficiently for Them to Perform Well

Because school is a microcosm of society, society's functions and problems are mirrored in the school. Compared to when most teachers were pupils themselves, there has been a dramatic increase in the divorce rate, resulting in fewer family and personal ties, and there has been an increase in family mobility and material affluence. Also, shifts toward cultural pluralism have brought with it less attention to conformity to a single set of values and at least a growing reluctance to use uniform and consistent standards to evaluate other's behavior. Another change has been that women have been taking their places in the labor force both as a result of a general emphasis on identity for women through careers and as a result of financial necessity in inflationary or economically unstable times.

In addition, the parents of the children now in school grew up in the post World War II affluence and went through the radical cultural dislocations of the end of the 20th century. They have always experienced a world with instant communications, through the media of television and the Internet, and have been exposed to a wide range of possibilities for leading one's life. The result of these forces seems to have been to increase the pace of life, with more parents oriented toward striving for material affluence often as a substitute for other unmet needs. These parents appear to be much more able to give children material comforts but less able to give them time and the personal contact and attention necessary to help them gain satisfaction in learning. The children reflect their parent's anxiety and lack of attention by seeking immediate gratification and attention (Berlin, 1964). Because of this diminished quality of relationships at home, it seems fewer and fewer children are coming to school ready and willing to gain satisfaction from learning.

Parents' relationships and attitudes toward the school have also changed. On the one hand, as a reaction to the uncertainty and alienation in their lives, parents have turned over to the schools much of the responsibility for rearing their children. It seems that parents have felt a loss in effectiveness and control over their children; they turn to the school in the hope that others may have more success. On the other hand, public faith in public education is obviously at a low point. The tax revolt has left the schools underfunded and other social service agencies bankrupt. Discussions of charter schools and the voucher system convey the attitude that schools are mismanaged by incompetents. As a result it has become harder and harder for teachers to garner cooperation from parents in helping children learn.

Given these sets of circumstances, the consultant can help in at least two ways: by helping the teacher increase parent conferencing skills and by focusing directly on the teacher's role. The first step is to make certain that the teacher has the skills on hand to elicit parental cooperation and support. Assured of this, and assuming no further progress with the client and client's family, the consultant then needs to explore with the consultee the parameters of the teacher's role. If the teacher has done all that can be done, that is, all that is within her role as a teacher, then the teacher needs to accept these limits. Sometimes just using authoritative support (Sarason, Levine, Goldenberg, Cherlin, & Bennett, 1966) helps the teacher accept the limits with less guilt and self-recrimination thereby freeing energy to work within those limits.

Curriculum Objectives and Materials for Children Are Irrelevant or Unrealistic

One of the main points made by Sarason in *The Culture of the School and the Problem of Change* is that many innovations are introduced into the schools without the knowledge, input, or contribution of those who must implement them. A continuing aspect of today's schools is the existence of fads and fashions in curriculum. Hucksters, legislators, professional organizations, college professors, and others find the schools easy vehicles to introduce new ideas and methods. Many of these additions to curriculum are very worthwhile and carefully thought through but there is a real human tendency to add new elements to the curriculum without taking elements away. Or, as Sarason (1990) points out, adding to or taking away from a system or systems that do not work without changing the system is a recipe for failure. In many cases, lessons, units, and whole subjects are added to the teacher's objectives for the year with no compensating permission to drop a corresponding amount of content. Teachers feel pressure to spread themselves thin and introduce lessons for the sake of being able to say they have covered the material, even though they realize that their time might be better spent covering a more limited amount of material in depth.

Another allied problem is that the concept of individual differences in children is given only lip service in most educational planning. The goal of getting all or most of the children to grade level by the end of the year does not make a great deal of sense in that the concept of grade level references norms. In test score norms, a grade equivalent for a particular score on the test is the score equal to the average score of children at a particular time during their schooling. As an average on a distribution of scores is typically normal in shape, approximately 50% of the children will score below the average or grade level. Yet often a teacher is shocked and horrified to learn that half the classroom scored below grade level, for such a record will be equated with failure as a teacher.

In other classrooms one hears the challenge that pupils should make one year's growth for one year's instruction. Unfortunately, a year's growth is also a normative statement and half the children would be expected to make more than a year's growth and half less.

In any case, teachers feel like they are on a production line with unrealistic quotas and are held accountable for many instructional units that are extraneous to what they perceive to be their pupil's most vital needs. The group norms for performance in the school system are quite unrealistic; nevertheless, most teachers have internalized them. The consultant must deal with the fact that the teachers do feel some pressure to meet these standards even though they may complain. The consultant can help by assisting teachers to examine the validity of these norms and the consequence of not being able to meet them for all of their pupils.

Many Children Are Unprepared or Unready for Instruction at Grade Level

There is a tendency among educators to displace blame downward. Because so much learning is hierarchical (Gagne, 1985) and builds upon what has already been learned, if the previous instruction was deficient in any way, a pupil will be unable to proceed with learning. If a previous teacher inadequately covered a topic or skill, or if the child did not master the concept for another reason, it is difficult for a teacher to take the time to review the topic satisfactorily for the handful of children who need it. Often the necessary resource materials are not conveniently available and the teacher is not practiced in covering the basic skill. Then too, the exact hierarchy of skills is not always clear to a teacher and although it is obvious that a child lacks some prerequisite skills, the determination of exactly which one is often beyond the ability of the teacher. As a result, one hears college professors pointing to the high school when they read an ungrammatical sentence in a student's essay, high school teachers attributing poor spelling to shoddy junior high or elementary-level instruction, junior high mathematics teachers pointing out with horror that a child cannot do simple long division, a skill learned in elementary school, and so on down to the kindergarten teacher who points out that a child is not ready for school. The fact is readiness for instruction, whether it is determined by biology or curriculum, is an individual difference and not all children will be able to benefit from instruction that is too advanced.

With pupil mobility and the resultant gaps that are left by moves from school to school, the individual differences in children's previous learning do present a difficult task for the teacher to address. The consultant can support the teacher in appreciating the enormity of the task and the fact that the system, too, recognizes the problem and has made provisions in the form of remedial and special education teachers to help with the task. Nevertheless, the consultant must help the teacher focus on what can be done in the immediate situation.

There Is Too Much Paperwork and Record Keeping

Starting with attendance and moving through the writing of lesson plans and yearly objectives, there is no doubt that the modern teacher has more clerical tasks to perform than ever before. On top of the regular record keeping, the teacher who does attempt to individualize instruction or to create a behavior modification or engineered classroom must spend what seems like inordinate amounts of time creating materials and record forms. In addition, many federal and state programs such as compensatory education, aimed at particularly difficult populations to teach, require extra evaluation in the form of questionnaires and test results from the teacher. To the extent that the schools have become a bureaucracy, the concomitant paperwork has added to the teacher's burden and represents a task that takes time away from other valuable activities.

The consultant's job in dealing with this reality is to attempt to understand with the teacher the purposes behind much of the record keeping and to empathize with the teacher about the tediousness of such work. Chores are much more easily done when it is clear what contributions they make to an ongoing enterprise and when one feels understood. Finding time to observe children's behavior and graph it as part of establishing a baseline for intervention is only one more task for the teacher.

Teachers Lack Administrative Sanction to Teach in Desired Ways

Many teachers are quite forthright in explaining that to the extent they are evaluated at all by the principal, it is clear that the administrator has some favored techniques, methods, and procedures. If the teacher does not use these sanctioned ways of teaching or managing a classroom, life can become very unpleasant in a school. It has been pointed out that principals and supervisors are not particularly accurate raters of teacher effectiveness but it is their role in the system. One might speculate that if administrators are not rating effective teaching behaviors, then they must be evaluating teachers on some other dimension, such as their personal notions of what good teaching is, or on other facets of observable behavior, such as interpersonal conduct away from the classroom, politics, and so on. It may be that because administrators have been successful teachers themselves, they rate teachers on how closely their behavior approximates the administrator's own teaching behavior and practices.

The relationship between the administrator and the teacher is most important (Hoy & DiPaola, 2010). Where the school climate and support system is good, teachers teach more effectively. What makes for a good administrative school climate is not as clear, but where the teachers feel free to make many decisions on their own and contribute to the making of other decisions that affect their life in the classroom, teachers seem to have better morale (Sarason, 1971). The consultant must realize that the teacher will feel powerless to act in many situations when it is felt that the administrator is not willing to back the teacher in any way. It becomes important as a consultant to help the teacher test the reality of the perceived sanctions that are operating in the school and even to help the teacher think about how to deal with the principal if need be.

Some Children Are Simply Out of Place in the Classroom

What teachers mean when they say that a child does not belong is that some children in the class are so extreme in their behavior, lack of skill, emotional maladjustment, and so on, that teachers become stressed when trying to accommodate them in the standard classroom. This view has been vindicated over the years with the growth of special education programs designed to serve children with special needs. But just like Mickey Mouse's broom "helpers" with the caldron of water in the "Sorcerer's Apprentice" from *Fantasia*, it seems like the more children are pulled from the classroom for special education, the more children appear in need of service. The number of children in need may indeed be increasing (as mentioned in the section on families, many more children may not be emotionally ready for the demands of school), but at the same time teachers have become more sensitive to children's needs and are able to identify more children than before.

Whatever the case, the consultant must be ready to acknowledge that a child or children in a classroom may be legitimate candidates for special help and must be ready to assist the teacher in securing that intervention for the child. Meanwhile, it should be made clear to teachers that one of the more effective treatments for emotionally disturbed, as well as all children, is success in a learning environment. Until a placement can be made for a client, the consultant and teacher must work out a way to provide educationally relevant, successful curriculum experiences for the child.

Teachers Have Unrealistic Professional Self-Expectations

The external environment and social structures are sources that act on teachers and must be considered by consultants. Another source is the teacher's set of subjective internal realities from which attitudes and expectations about teaching come. Some of these attitudes can be traced back to how they were prepared as teachers. The apprenticeship model of teacher preparation still predominates. Teachers learn to teach primarily by observation and imitation. They take courses on curriculum materials and methods but get very little grounding on well-formulated models of the teaching and learning process. They learn many techniques and procedures, and tricks of the trade, but not how the methods they are learning are related to the process of learning in children. In Sarason's terms, they learn a number of the existing programmatic and behavioral regularities along with the intended outcome of these. Seldom are the actual outcomes explored and rarely is there a rationale for how the regularities produce the intended outcomes.

"Children" seem to be the missing topic in teacher education and few teachers arrive at a working knowledge of individual differences in child development. Courses in educational psychology are not well integrated into the curriculum and are often criticized as irrelevant. Even when courses in educational psychology are integral parts of teacher education, the focus in these courses is on learning theory, child development theory, and tests and measurements. Seldom do these courses touch on the affective nature of the classroom or on the emotional component of the teacher's life.

The Administrator's Position in the School System

Administrators can be consultees or may need to sanction and support an intervention generated in consultation. Consultants must understand the important position they hold in the system. Since administrators are almost always former teachers, they bring with them to their positions most of the attitudes and perceptions of the system that they cultivated as teachers. Moreover, administrators typically move into their position after being selected from the ranks of good teachers where they have demonstrated an ability to adapt to the system and have embraced the prevailing attitudes about how schools should operate. Administrators are often not specifically prepared for their role, with training often coming after an administrative appointment and consisting of academic, largely theoretical coursework (Sarason, 1971). When administrators are asked the same question as teachers (What prevents you from doing your job more effectively?), they give many of the same replies as teachers. Certainly they would concur that the home environments of children get in the way of schooling but they add to the list a number of reasons. School administrators often mention the following impediments.

There Are Too Many Laws, Rules, and Regulations Constraining the Freedom of Action in Schools

Although the teacher perceives the administrator as having a great deal of power in most situations, the administrator in turn feels bound by numerous laws or district-level regulations. Sarason notes that an important variable in the effectiveness of a principal is the degree of the sense that one's fate is in one's own hands and is internally controlled rather than controlled by the system. Nevertheless, it is true that a bewildering array of laws ranging from the reporting of child abuse or the administration of corporal punishment, to legislation requiring that topics such as substance abuse prevention be included in the curriculum do exist, and it is the administrator's duty to see to it that these regulations are followed. The fear of legal action and the expense it can incur is extraordinarily strong in most school people.

The consultant must realize that these fears and concerns on the part of administrators are not groundless. Administrators are the ones legally responsible for what takes place at school. Districts are targets for litigation and it is most important that due process be followed in many procedures, in spite of the time and expense, in order to ensure that the limited funds of the district be protected from suit. Administrators do need help, however, in reexamining how the current practices operate to comply with regulations or how the intent of laws gets translated into school procedures. The administrator is responsible, ultimately, and cannot ignore legal constraints.

There Is Far Too Much Paperwork

Related to the first reason for difficulty, because many reports and other paperwork are required by law, the administrator's role necessarily involves a great deal of time for budget planning and otherwise expediting the solution of the physical needs of the school. Administrators must see to the food for the children's lunch; the books, papers, and pencils that are used in the classroom; and everything else that is in use around the school. The administrator must estimate needs, conduct inventories, and report to others what is occurring in the school. In order to meet goals and deadlines for paperwork, administrators spend a great deal of time learning about new regulations and in meetings making group decisions with peers. These housekeeping tasks are enormous and do consume a great deal of time. There is no doubt that effort spent in this manner does take effort away from other possible activities, particularly in working with and supporting teachers.

Again the consultant must recognize the legitimacy of an administrator's explanation that paperwork gets in the way. Few administrators understand when they start out how much of their job will be routine clerical work. This does not mean that there may not be ways to reduce this workload through the delegation of authority and decentralization. Although the consultant can help administrators look at these possibilities, paperwork is a necessary and enduring part of the administrator's role and does take time away from the role of educational leader.

Most Teachers Do Not Perceive Administrators as Helpful and Are Threatened by Them

School administrators find themselves in a real bind because their role has two seemingly incompatible elements. Administrators are to be supervisors and resources for teachers to use in times of difficulty on the one hand, and are to be monitors and evaluators of their work in the classroom, on the other. In general, administrators want to establish cooperative, friendly coordinate relationships with teachers yet have the power to make personal decisions that can markedly affect the teachers' careers. For the beginning teacher who is usually most in need of wise council from an experienced hand at the school, the evaluations surrounding the granting of tenure are extraordinarily threatening. It is the building administrator who is the key person involved in the decision. Even after tenure has been earned, there are still decisions over which the administrator has influence that can make life in the classroom pleasant or miserable, such as the assignment of classrooms, the make-up of a class, and the grade level assigned. Few administrators have the skill to help teachers to be comfortable when they are present in the classroom, even when the stated reason is to offer help to the teachers. To ask for help in our society is often interpreted as weakness and teachers are often not willing to take a chance on the ability of the principal or other administrator to divorce the roles of evaluator and supervisor. Instead they prefer to be let alone and the administrator soon senses that a barrier to effective communication has been erected. Levine (1972) pointed out, however, that a skillful principal can be an effective collaborator with teachers if trained to do so.

The consultant must realize that the administrator would like to serve in a role very much like that of the consultant. In fact, they may be jealous and feel threatened by the consultant's relationship with the teachers, for they believe they should have such access to teachers. Consultants must be able to help the administrator understand why they are not always welcome in the classroom and deal with the frustration that this brings about in the administrator. Although it is possible for administrators to improve their acceptability in the classroom, they will never be able to overcome the anxiety they arouse in teachers by virtue of their position.

Teachers Are Not Able to Manage Children Properly; Administrators Spend Too Much Time "Cleaning Up" after Them

Many administrators, particularly elementary school principals, can spend whole days doing nothing but punishing children sent to their office and calling their parents. Usually these are children in crisis who may have been fighting or who are otherwise out of control of their behavior and thus cannot be ignored or seen at the administrator's convenience. Dealing with problems from the classroom is annoying and requires a great deal of energy. With some justification, administrators reason that if teachers were doing a more effective job, they would prevent many or most of the incidents that escalate into emergencies. Although discipline is the most common specific complaint, there are other tasks that fall to administrators as a result of others in the school not performing competently or through simple human error. Principals, for example, may find themselves substitute teaching, driving a child to a medical appointment, chaperoning a school dance, or doing any number of things that any number of other people could do just as well.

If the discipline problem becomes too extreme, the consultant may need to help the administrator think through what is occurring that creates this number of distractions and diversions. The administrator may need help in developing more or better skills to help teachers cope with these kinds of problems, or he or she may need support in accepting the evaluative role wherein it is appropriate to censure or redirect others who have not been doing their job. Nevertheless, many demands coming from crisis will always be there for administrators and the consultant must see them as legitimate parts of the administrator's job. The administrator has ultimate responsibility for what occurs within the school and is often the last line of defense when things break down. This backup capacity may get in the way of performing other important tasks around the school.

Administrators Have Difficulty Being Leaders Because They Are Often Caught in the Middle of Countervailing Forces

Administrators often feel stymied because they are caught in the middle of many factions: children, teachers, parents, other administrators, and the school board. Their loyalties on many issues may be completely divided and they end up being paralyzed in taking any action. They have become administrators by virtue of subscribing to the values of the system, yet they realize that to do their job they must attend to what is best for children and the needs of their staff. In addition, all of the factions demand that the administrator become their ally. The concept of community control implies that the administrator should be a representative for the parents or the neighborhood. The concept of the school staff as a group of professionals implies that the administrator is a representative of the teachers or is a head teacher. The concept of educational leader makes the administrator a child advocate, and the concept of the school as a system places the administrator as part of an organization that has established goals. Because administrators subscribe to all these concepts, they perceive themselves as unable to be neutral arbiters and decision makers. They recognize the need for cooperation and democratic action between all members if the school is to function effectively.

In particular, as Sarason points out, administrators view "the System" as being very conservative and rigid in wishing the status quo to remain the same. Whether this is true or not, and Sarason argues that it likely is not, administrators are loath to "make waves" and believe it is necessary to follow directives from above without question. At the same time, they realize they are thereby forced to fit Procrustean beds of policy that may not fit their particular local situation. With this feeling of helplessness, it becomes impossible to take decisive steps toward solving problems.

The consultant is obliged to reflect and appreciate the administrator's sense of being pulled in many directions. At the same time, for the schools to function, the administrator must stop weighing all of the considerations when a decision is to be made, and must take a position. Consultants can help the principal clarify and set priorities for issues and then can supply the needed support in recognizing that decisions must be made, even if some people will be unhappy as a result.

Considering the Context for Interventions

With all these constraints acting on teachers and administrators, one question the consultant might ask is, "what factors characterize effective schools?" Five important characteristics are (a) strong educational leadership from the principal; (b) high expectations of student achievement; (c) an emphasis on basic skills; (d) a safe and orderly climate; and (e) frequent evaluation of pupil progress on achievement (Reynolds, Creemers, Stringfield, Teddlie, & Schaffer, 2002). Children learn in such environments, and behavioral problems may be minimized since children are engaged. With these characteristics in mind, the consultant and consultee can evaluate strategies for the consultee to address the client's issues in light of healthy system attributes.

At the same time they need to assess how potential interventions will work with the teacher's attitudes and understandings operating in the client's classroom as well as classroom constraints such as time and logistical problems. The intervention will also have to work in a school where administrator attitudes and understandings are set, and where school climate and resources may be compromised. The consultant and consultee must be realistic about what is feasible in the current setting. There will be an imperative to consider evidence-based interventions that have been shown to work with similar clients, but these interventions will have to be adapted or modified for the particular setting or discarded as impractical.

Guidelines for Analyzing and Considering the Context for Intervention

Interpersonal-Behavioral

a) Explore the attitudes and values of the personnel in the school including the consultee.
b) Explore the relationship between the consultee and the client's parents.
c) Consider laws, rules, and regulations that constrain freedom of action.

Intrapersonal-Cerebral

a) Determine the organizational culture of this school setting.
b) Assess the administrator's capacity to support innovation in this school.
c) Evaluate the kind of relationship that exists between the teacher and administrators.

Self-Monitoring Questions

a)   Have I helped identify constraints operating in this school on the use of any interventions chosen?

b)   How feasible will it be to make changes in this classroom and school?

c)   How much flexibility will this teacher consultee and I have to implement a given intervention?

d)   How many other children in this setting share the client's problem?

e)   Have we identified all of the social and environmental forces at work that have created this situation?

f)   What are the limits on the teacher concerning what can physically or temporarily be done during the day?

g)   Is there any task the consultee can safely drop to take on an additional chore?

h)   How much support does this consultee have from those above and below the administrative hierarchy?

i)   Given that there are environmental forces causing children to have difficulties in school, how can I best get the consultee to accept that some productive efforts at helping can be made at school?

j)   How free is this consultee to experiment with the teacher or administrator role—where is the locus of control for the consultee?

k)   Have we considered what group phenomena are occurring in the classroom?

References

Berlin, I.N. (1960). The theme in mental health consultation sessions. *American Journal of Orthopsychiatry, 30,* 827–228.

Berlin, I.N. (1964). Learning mental health consultation history and problems. *Mental Hygiene, 48,* 257–266.

Gagne, R.M. (1985). *The conditions of learning and theory of instruction.* Belmont, CA: Wadsworth.

Gallessich, J. (1982). *The profession and practice of consultation.* San Francisco: Jossey-Bass Publishers.

Hoy, W.K., & DiPaola, M. (Eds.). (2010). *Analyzing school contexts: Influences of principals and teachers in the service of students.* Charlotte, NC: IAP Information Age Publishing.

Levine, M. (1972). The practice of mental health consultation: Some definitions from social theory. In J. Zusman & D.L. Davidson (Eds.), *Practical aspects of mental health consultation* (pp. 9–29). Springfield, IL: Charles E. Thomas.

Reynolds, D., Creemers, B., Stringfield, S., Teddlie, C., & Schaffer, G. (2002). *World class schools: International perspectives on school effectiveness.* London: Routledge Falmer.

Sandoval, J. (1977) Mental health consultation for teachers in preservice training. *California Journal of Teacher Education, 3,* 110–124.

Sarason, S.B. (1971). *The culture of the school and the problem of change.* New York: Teachers College Press.

Sarason, S.B. (1990). *The predictable failure of educational reform: Can we change course before it is too late?* San Francisco: Jossey-Bass.

Sarason, S.B. (1996). *Revisiting "The culture of the school and the problem of change."* New York: Teachers College Press.

Sarason, S.B., Levine, M., Goldenberg, I.I., Cherlin, D.L., & Bennett, E.M. (1966). *Psychology in community settings: Clinical educational, vocational, social aspects.* New York: John Wiley.

Schmuck, R.A., & Runkle, P.J. (1984). *The handbook of organization development in schools and colleges.* Prospect Heights, IL: Waveland Press.

Schmuck, R.A., & Schmuck, P. (2000). *Group processes in the classroom* (8th ed.). Boston: McGraw Hill.

8

GENERATING INTERVENTIONS IN CONSULTATION

This chapter focuses on interventions generated during the course of consultation. In many ways, consultation itself is an intervention since it is a variation in the routine of the consultee's life and may bring about change simply through the process itself. Talking about a problem with the consultant may be enough to bring relief to the consultee. Hylander (2004) calls this phenomenon a magic turning, when, following a consultation session, the consultee's relationship with the client improves without an obvious change in conceptualization or behavior. The change in relationship may come about as a result of the discharge of anxiety and emotion that occurs in the process of talking openly about a problem, or in subtle insights that come to mind during a dialogue. After the first session with the consultant, the consultee may simply be more relaxed around the client and the client responds favorably.

The word *intervention* means something new occurring in an existing system. In this context, intervention means imposing a change in an already ongoing situation so as to improve functioning between the consultee and client. Simply put, an intervention is a new idea or conceptualization that results in a change in the consultee's professional activities and a parallel change in the client. Consultees look for new ideas when coming to consultation and seek interventions to alleviate professional problems.

One might think that this would be one of the first topics covered in a book on consultation but the delay in discussing this topic is for a reason. As a novice consultant, one is most concerned about being useful when a consultee brings a problem up. For the consultee, the problem is real and usually there is an emergency or crisis sense to the meeting. The consultee comes to consultation with the expectation of advice and suggestions, and the fantasy that the consultant will offer a clear and effective directive with a minimum of fuss. The consultant wants to meet this expectation and to be helpful by coming up with one or more ideas for them to use in addressing the presented problem. This is, of course, an "expert" model of consultation and the novice consultant and consultee are often seduced into believing that the consultant should draw on experience and accumulated wisdom to produce a solution to the difficulty. Before generating interventions, however, the consultee-centered consultant must avoid taking hasty action and determine that the time is right.

By this point, the reader has come to view consultation as a process, and appreciates that it is important for a peer relationship to develop in consultation rather than an authority relationship (Guvå, 2004). A nonhierarchical stance functions to make "it emotionally easier for a consultee to choose to adopt and internalize the consultant's less inhibited and more hopeful view of the client's situation. The nonhierarchical relationship also encourages free expression without fear of disparagement" (Caplan-Moskovich & Caplan, 2004, p. 195). The consultant should not proceed to developing interventions until the consultee is truly ready for this stage, and the problem has been adequately clarified. This latter point is particularly important because as problems are first described, the consultant may have tentative solutions that may jump to mind. It is tempting to throw them onto the table before verifying that the perceived problem is the primary difficulty. An intervention for the wrong problem will not be useful. If part of the temptation is to offer ideas to the consultee for fear of forgetting them, the consultant might wish to jot down a note to him or herself, rather than interrupt the client too soon.

The offering of suggestions for intervention should only occur after the consultant and consultee have created a working hypothesis about what forces are operating in the problem situation. The creation of a hypothesis comes about slowly after the collection of data from discussion, observation, the review of records, interviews, and other activities. The consultant and the consultee should be trying to create a mental picture of the dynamic of the problem. It is not necessary that both the consultee and the consultant create exactly the same conceptualization but ultimately the two views of the situation should be somewhat similar or alternate hypotheses should be at least acknowledged.

Another issue concerning timing of interventions is to proceed only when the consultee's emotions have been addressed. Strong emotions can impede creativity and foreclose some options for action that may be appropriate.

Before Offering Suggestions

Two Key Questions

Prior to the point where the consultant starts offering some suggestions or ideas that might be turned into interventions, two key questions should be part of the consultation dialogue. These are both "stock" questions that frequently come up in consultation. They are "What have you done already to address this problem?" and "What have you done with other children in situations in the past similar to this one?" A variant question is What do other teachers do (or have done) with such a problem (child)? These questions have been discussed in other chapters.

The first question, "What have you done so far?" helps the consultant avoid what is called "the suggestion game," or the kind of dialogue where the consultant throws out a suggestion only to have the consultee respond with "I've already tried that (and it didn't work)." Although this game can be satisfying to the consultee, in that it makes the consultant seem not particularly innovative and frustrates the consultant so the consultant can share the affect associated with failure, it ultimately is not productive. After the consultee states that a strategy has been tried during a dialogue, it is often difficult to get the strategy reconsidered again in consultation. If, however, the interventions tried are asked about, or the consultee brings them up, they can be reviewed carefully and possibly reconsidered because they were not competently executed or were not tried for a long enough time; that is, implemented with integrity. In addition, when the consultee reviews the steps already taken to address the situation, the consultant can acknowledge the consultee's creativity and ability to take initiative.

Another advantage to finding out what has already been done is to avoid repeating a mistake. Often learning what has not worked also throws light onto the underlying forces creating the situation.

Asking what has worked with other children or for other teachers in analogous circumstances often has powerful effects. Sometimes such a question helps by taking the focus off the particular child and the teacher-consultee will know about some successful interventions that have worked with similar children but somehow have not been recalled or seen as applying in this case. The question can simply bridge the gap between this case and other cases where the consultee has been successful. Another advantage is that if an intervention has been successful for the consultee previously it may work again. Success is not guaranteed, but chances are that the intervention tried is one the consultee is competent with and finds to be acceptable, and these are important features in an intervention (Witt & Elliott, 1985).

Although exploring what the consultee has done previously is useful for a variety of reasons, it may not lead to an intervention. If it does not, the consultant may still feel pressure to offer a suggestion, particularly when nothing comes to mind. In such a situation, one of the hardest, but one of the most useful, things to say is "I don't know."

The Feared "I Don't Know"

One of the advantages of saying "I don't know" when a consultant is called upon to offer a suggestion of what to do, is that it acknowledges that the problem is a difficult one. Being too facile and too quick with an answer may make the consultant look good, but it does imply that complex human problems have simple solutions, which is usually not the case. Not being sure is realistic in most situations, and we should always try to foster the experimental attitude.

The consultant should use the phrase honestly, of course. It is certainly better to admit puzzlement rather than to bluff it out. On the one hand, one should not say, "I don't know" when one has a good idea to share. On the other hand, if it is a truthful statement, it has the virtue of demonstrating that the consultant is human and can admit the fact when a difficult problem is faced. In Carl Rogers's terms, it is a way of demonstrating that the consultant is genuine and congruent. In social learning terms, it is a way of modeling openness of communication.

Another effect of saying "I don't know" is that it restores the peer relationship in consultation. It is a form of one-downsmanship in that it avoids the consultant taking an expert role, dispensing knowledge and wisdom. The phrase helps to create a partnership or a team approach to problem solving. The consultant says, in effect, "I don't know, you don't know, but maybe together we can come up with a solution—I don't *know* but we can try." Saying "I don't know" or "we will have to try some things to see what works" emphasizes that this problem is unusual and is one that is going to require some work and some effort, and takes the problem out of the routine category. Saying otherwise communicates that this problem is trivial and a formula intervention will work.

In many instances saying "I don't know" fosters the experimental attitude. When we admit we don't know, we turn a situation into a mystery to be solved. With a mystery, we look for clues, generate hypotheses, and do experiments to come up with a theory to test. These tests become the interventions.

It goes without saying that the consultant will not often say "I don't know." Overuse or inappropriate use of the phrase will make the consultant seem like someone with nothing to contribute or a fatalist. Some consultees who have naive views of the process may not accept it. Still, consultants should feel free to admit when they are stumped or when they are out of ideas.

Approaches to Intervention Generation for the Client

It is useful to distinguish between two approaches to generating ideas and suggestions in consultation for understanding and intervening with the client. No doubt consultants use both. Generating interventions is thinking at a very high level and involves both convergent production and divergent production. It is difficult to describe or foster a consultant's creativity. Nevertheless, a consultant may either resort to a "tricks of the trade," "best practice," or prescriptive approach to interventions or resort to a theory-based approach.

Prescriptive Intervention

Once one of the most popular texts in the field of school psychology, Ralph Blanco's *Prescriptions for Children with Learning and Adjustment Problems* (Blanco,

1972) was the first cataloging of possible interventions for particular problems encountered in the classroom. This volume contains a list of interventions that have been found to be effective with dealing with a number of child problems in the school. For each problem, Blanco has collected and evaluated a number of interventions suggested by school psychologist practitioners or other experts. An example of a prescription is, "praise the child when completes his worksheet with 90% accuracy." Blanco's method to generate the book was to send out questionnaires to practitioners in the field and to ask them how they would deal with an issue. The interventions are listed by age of applicability, rating of effectiveness, and likelihood of success, and for whom the intervention is made. The book is a compilation of his results.

The consultant using this book as a reference might look up the interventions associated with the problem. The consultant using such a resource would probably be familiar with most of the ideas, but might encounter new ideas or be reminded of interventions not brought to mind and out of awareness. The book is, then, a bag of tricks, a list of what works. Over a lifetime a consultant would pick up a number of interventions that are specific to the kinds of problems they encounter. Beginning consultants might use a modern equivalent of Blanco's book or turn to peers or supervisors.

There is no one theoretical approach represented in Blanco's book. The prescriptions listed are present by virtue of their effectiveness. Most school psychologists would describe themselves as eclectic pragmatists and are not bothered by a listing of prescriptions.

Blanco's work was not the only source for prescriptions. Jeff Grimes, a State School Psychology Consultant in Iowa, produced a volume called *Psychological Approaches to Problems of Children and Adolescents* (Grimes, 1982). Experts on a number of topics created short chapters on specific problems and different interventions to help children in school. Chapters offer ideas on such issues as children coping with divorce, counseling the homosexual adolescent, runaways, enuresis, truancy, and so on.

Over the years, The National Association of School Psychologists has published a similar volume, now in its fifth edition with a sixth on the way, entitled *Best Practices in School Psychology* (Thomas & Grimes, 1997). Although each chapter in *Best Practices* contains a theoretical and research review on the issue, the intent is to document best practice for intervention. Some of the topics covered are social skills training, discipline referrals, school climate, and so on.

With the move to evidence-based practice, volumes are now appearing that explicitly state the evidence on which a program or intervention strategy is based (e.g., Vannest, Reynolds, & Kamphaus, 2008). Websites containing established interventions are also available. Two prominent sites are Intervention Central (www.interventioncentral.org) and the What Works Clearinghouse (http://ies .ed.gov/ncee/wwc/).

A consultant, then, can in the course of consultation, review resources such as these and have a clear justification for various interventions, as well as a number of new ideas to try. With experience, the consultant will have accumulated a personal set of "tricks" or best practices.

Theory-Based Interventions

An alternative to the prescriptive approach is generating interventions from evidence-based theory. If a topic is not covered in one of the resources listed above, and none of the ideas can be adapted to the current situation, or if the consultant does not have time to consult a literature review and must generate ideas on the spot, it is possible to turn to psychological theory for inspiration. Consultants should have a considerable body of theory at their disposal from their study of psychology. They have most likely had courses in developmental psychology, learning, and social psychology, as well as other fields that can help them generate interventions.

What the consultant must do in thinking about a problem is to frame the problem or situation from one or more psychological points of view. The consultant asks, for example, what do theories of emotional development say about this problem and do these theories suggest an intervention. Rather than proceeding from a type of problem and what empirical data or folklore would suggest works for that specific difficulty, the consultant reviews theory in general as it might apply to the problem.

It is impossible in this text to review all of the psychological theory that may have application to the kinds of problems children have in school and the kinds of problems schools have in being effective. We can, by way of example, examine some broad concepts from a number of theoretical domains that can be used in generating interventions or helping conceptualize a problem.

Developmental Theory

One of the first questions the consultant asks the consultee when the subject of concern is a child is how old that child is. Central to all developmental theory is the notion that children go through a progression of stages roughly correlated with age. Our conception of "normal" behavior in children is often based on what is age appropriate. Individual differences in children are often attributed to differences in maturity suggesting that not all children of a particular age are at the same stage. A related idea is that not all children are at the same level of development in different domains. A child's physical status may not be related to his intellectual or emotional status and a child often is at a different stage in different domains.

In addition to helping a consultant evaluate the status of the child and to bring an understanding of what is "normal" and what is not, developmental concepts lead to interventions by suggesting what the appropriate developmental task for the child is and by suggesting how development might be facilitated.

If a child is at a particular stage, theory usually suggests that that specific stage must be mastered before moving on, and that the child will progress one stage at a time. Knowing with some likelihood what the next stage will be helps the consultant and consultee to arrange developmentally appropriate experiences for the child at home and at school.

How development may be facilitated or speeded up, what Piaget called "The American Question," has been the subject of long debate. To generalize, it seems that presenting the child with information or experience that is slightly more advanced developmentally and then giving him or her a chance to work (or play) with the challenge can facilitate movement. For example, a child with egocentric reasoning about a moral dilemma may be given alternative reasoning about the problem that is principle based. Through exposure and discussion with others, growth in moral reasoning may occur. This idea of structured exposure to the next level of thought is also at the heart of Vygotski's conceptualization of the zone of proximal development.

Psychodynamic Theory

Freud's theories, particularly his ideas about emotional development in children, are not popular in many quarters and have largely been superseded by other theorists such as Erik Erikson. Nevertheless, a number of Freud's ideas, particularly concerned with the workings of the ego system still have great currency. Perhaps Freud's greatest contribution to psychology is the concept of unconscious motivation. Freud discovered that mental life is far more complex than what is in our awareness. Defense mechanisms operate to alter our perception of the world and actions can result from patterns and experiences from the past that we do not easily recognize.

Freud's theories have always had implications for interventions because of his work as a psychotherapist. Freud's interventions have been encapsulated in the "talking" cure where, simply put, a relationship with the therapist has been used as a forum discovering hidden motivation and working through long-standing conflicts that interfere with adaptive functioning in the present. With children, this relationship often takes the form of play therapy.

Psychotherapy is seldom a practical intervention in consultation, although referring a child or others to outside therapists is fairly common. Instead, interventions in the classroom are more likely to focus on conceptualizing a child as having complex needs and motives for his behaviors and searching for more acceptable outlets or ways of expressing his needs in the school, family, or other milieu. In recognizing that a child's subjective reality is more pertinent than the reality perceived by others, modifications can be made to accommodate the child's reality. For example, if a young boy's behavior of provoking adults to intervene and restrain him appears, after thought, to be a function of a fear of being out of control, the consultant and consultee can search for other ways of addressing the child's fear that are more appropriate in the classroom.

Another offshoot of psychodynamic thinking is attachment theory. Attachment theory concerns later social relationships that develop as a result of the initial closeness in the relationship between caregivers and infants (Ainsworth, 1969). Understanding and responding to a child's need for secure attachment can guide intervention.

Social Learning Theory

In the past several decades, social learning theory has been extremely influential in helping teachers and others intervene in children's lives to facilitate learning and development. The key concepts in behavioral learning theory are that all behaviors have antecedents, and are followed by consequences or reinforcements. Changing behaviors can come about by modifying stimuli and reinforcements so that undesired behaviors are extinguished and desired behaviors are appropriately reinforced. Since human beings are social animals, behavior change can take place through observation or self-control methods using social reinforcements. The technology of behavior change based on behavioral learning theory is vast, and a comprehensive school of consultation has developed based on this body of theory and research (cf. Bergan & Kratochwill, 1990).

In a nutshell, after a problem has been translated into behavioral terms by identifying a specific behavior to decelerate and a specific behavior to accelerate, the behaviorist (e.g., a teacher) carefully monitors the situation where either behavior is likely to occur, and works toward finding ways for rewards to be delivered. Behavioral consultation has a specific system for reaching this point, but any school-based consultant can draw on behavioral learning theory to design interventions. The consultant often asks "How would you like for this client to act differently?" so the focus in consultation can be on how to bring this new behavior about.

Cognitive Psychology

A rival to behavioral theory in explaining human learning is cognitive psychology. The central concept in cognitive psychology is the mental schema or the notion that through experience individuals build up a set of relationships between concepts, which must be reconciled with new learning. Learning does not take place in a vacuum but new experiences must be accommodated and assimilated into current mental structures. An individual's cognitive schema will be quite individual because of the uniqueness of each person's experience. In order to understand another person, we must learn how that individual understands the world and organizes new information. The individual's frame of reference is very important in predicting and explaining how new data will be processed.

Other aspects of cognitive psychology are an information processing view of the learning process, and an emphasis on learning hierarchies. The use of a computer as a model for learning makes use of concepts such as sensory register, short-term memory, long-term memory, and so on. The model can be of use to us in appreciating children's individual differences and in making changes in the classroom to accommodate a child's strengths and weaknesses (cf. Rosenfield, 1987).

Learning hierarchy, a concept dealt with in great detail in the writings of Robert Gagne (1985), is the notion that skills and competencies identified as outcomes in education can be broken down into prerequisite skills and competencies. The prerequisites in turn can be broken down, and so on until a learning hierarchy can be identified. Gagne wrote about the conditions of learning necessary for acquiring a type of learning in a hierarchy. Types of learning vary from simple s-r learning through complex problem solving and principle learning. A first hypothesis the consultant might test in encountering a client who does not behave in a particular way is that he or she lacks the prerequisite learning for the behavior. The solution, then, is to identify the skills lacking and to provide them.

Social Psychology

Social psychology is also a rich source of theory about why children function as they do in a school setting. Social psychologists, among other topics, study group process phenomenon and the formation of attitudes. A knowledge about normative processes, group influence and risk taking, cohesiveness and scapegoating, and leadership can be helpful in considering why children end up in particular roles in the classroom and have difficulty.

Knowing about attitudes about the self, be they general as in self-concept or particular as in attributions for academic success and failure, is also useful. In general, social psychology has taught us that to change attitudes, it is often effective to change behaviors. A careful attention to client and consultee attitudes can help to plan for behavior change that will result in more productive functioning.

Attribution theory also is particularly relevant. For example, a child who views his or her school success as attributable to internal, controllable, stable personal factors will perform very differently from another who attributes success to external, uncontrollable, unstable factors (chance). Interventions can be based on changing a child's attributions for success and failure.

Generalizations across Theories

Across all of these theoretical notions about the causes of children's behavior, there are at least three common themes or ideas. The first is that behavior results from a developmental process. In the academic domain an example is Gagne's notion of learning hierarchies. Current behavior is the result of mastering prerequisite skills. If a child is unable to do something, the first question to ask is whether the child has learned foundational behaviors. If not, focus on supplying the prerequisites and provide social support. Similar questions can be asked about emotional development (Freud) and social development.

A second generalization is that the behavior exists in an ecosystem. There are many forces acting to support and maintain a behavior. For change to occur, all of these supports must be identified and addressed if any intervention is to be sustained.

Finally, it is important to realize the existence of subjective reality. How an individual perceives things and organizes these perceptions influences subsequent behaviors. A child's theories about the self and others determine how he or she will act.

Intervening with the Consultee

Usually when we think about interventions we think about changes directed at the client. But the distinctive feature of consultee-centered consultation is that the process is also an intervention with the consultee. The consultant must listen carefully to determine to what extent each source of consultee difficulty is impacting the consultee's professional functioning. Such a determination is important since each implies a different approach to consultation. Intervening with the consultee is done through the consultation process itself. This topic has been covered in Chapter 2. The reader may review Table 2.1, which lists each of Caplan's four sources of consultee difficulty, descriptions for each one, signs of the difficulty during consultation, and the intervention strategies for dealing with it.

Creating Culturally Relevant Interventions

As the consultant and consultee work together to design a strategy to address the client's hypothesized problems, they must keep in mind the consultee's cultural background and level of acculturation. It may be necessary first to expand on the consultant and consultee's cultural awareness and competence.

Assuming they have sufficient information about the values, norms, beliefs, and traditions of the client, the consultant and consultee attempt to build on cultural strengths, remembering that they will also need to take into account the client's level of acculturation to the mainstream culture. They will also examine closely evidence-based practices that might be used, recognizing that any intervention will have to be adjusted for use with this client.

In reviewing the evidence supporting a particular intervention or practice, the consultant and consultee must ask with whom the intervention was used, who were the interventionists, and in what setting the intervention occurred. Interventions that have not been tested with diverse intervention recipients, interventionists, and settings are unknown in terms of their effectiveness with many groups. The consultee and consultant may need to adjust the intervention to make it meaningful and successful for different clients of a particular culture or in different

TABLE 8.1 Questions to ask when considering evidence about an intervention and possible transportation and adoption in a new setting (Ingraham & Oka, 2006).

Questions	Purpose
What are the similarities and differences between the people and context of the study vs. those of my work setting?	Assess the transferability and generalizability.
When there are differences, what modifications would best take into account the cultures of my intended setting?	Need to make adjustments to match the context and target population.
What is known about the mechanisms of change that make this intervention effective?	Sources of resistance or possible unanticipated outcomes.
How will I involve members of my target population in helping with implementation?	Participation from cultural resources or informants for additional planning.
What formative data will be used to evaluate how the intervention is working in the new setting and with the new groups of people?	Formative evaluation needed to decide early if intervention is working and if changes are needed.

contexts (e.g., with older or younger clients). Whether or not adjustments will affect the outcome of the intervention is an empirical question that will require the consultant and consultee to be extra careful in evaluating effectiveness through formative evaluation (Ingraham & Oka, 2006). Table 8.1 lists some questions to ask when considering evidence about an intervention and possible transportation and adoption in a new setting.

The Intervention Planning Conversation

Just because a consultee has expressed an intention to modify his or her behavior with the client does not mean they will follow through. Sanetti, Kratochwill, and Long (2013), based on Adult Behavior Change Theory, suggested that the consultant and consultee complete a pre-intervention implementation plan. The plan is a way to move from intention to intervene to effective action. The intervention plan (a) defines and lists the steps involved in the new strategy, (b) specifies adaptations that must be made to the strategy to fit the consultee's situation, (c) considers the logistics and timing of the strategy, (d) identifies resources and barriers to implementation, and (e) discusses how to cope with these obstacles.

The planning conversation should involve setting some goals for the consultee and client. Making these goals explicit will assist later in planning evaluation and providing a check on the likelihood of success of the selected intervention. At this point in the process the consultant and consultee will have settled on a working hypothesis. If there still remains an alternative hypothesis about the dynamics of the problem, it can also be considered as part of "plan B."

ɔssible interventions can usually be divided into *child-focused* versus *system-*
d. If the decision is that the problem resides within the child, it implies focusing on changes in the consultee's approach in the classroom. If there is thought
that systemic forces are contributing to the problem, some intervention may be
directed at changes in organizations or institutions. The consultant may have more
of a role in bringing administrators or parents into the conversation. Intervention
at both levels might be considered.

Often there is bias toward seeing the problem as residing solely in the client. Sometimes this bias is totally justified, and intervention in the school setting is impossible, as with psychotic children or children experiencing familial
abuse. Sometimes an intervention is to refer the case to an outside resource or
institution.

The consultee and consultant ultimately must choose what to do. The different
perspectives and ideas brought up during consultation can lead to more than one
intervention. How can we choose among them? Elsewhere, Davis and I proposed
the following criteria (Davis & Sandoval, 1991).

(a) The acceptability of the intervention to those responsible for intervention
implementation (Elliott, Witt, Galvin, & Peterson, 1984; Witt, 1986). The
individual who will intervene must understand the intervention, believe the
intervention has the potential to be effective, believe that they can make
the changes necessary for successful implementation, and have high motivation to follow through. The consultant will need to continue to check the
consultee's willingness to move forward.

(b) The likelihood of success. Some interventions are more likely to work than
others. Research has shown that some interventions are successful with
particular problems. Thus proven or validated rather than unproven interventions should be attempted. For example, modeling, rather than lectur-
ing should be used to promote preschooler's social skills (Elliott & Ershier,
1990). Further, most interventions come with assumptions that need validation. For example, if free time will be used as reinforcement for desired
behavior, it should be determined that the child does, in fact, value free
time.

(c) The effort or ease involved in intervening. School personnel have limited
time to devote to individual children. All other things being equal, one would
choose intervention requiring the least time expenditure.

(d) The probability of unanticipated outcomes and disruptions in other systems brought about by the intervention. Ecological theory suggests that any
change in a system will disrupt it in ways that are difficult to foresee. Nevertheless, one must ask if an intervention is likely to bring about an undesirable
outcome in the client or others (see e.g., Abidin, 1975).

(e) Ethical considerations. From time to time interventions are suggested that
violate ethical codes. For example, if an intervention requires violation of a

confidence, it must be rejected. The ethical implications of actions should be thought through.

(f) Urgency considerations. If it is determined that an emergency or crisis exists and that things will get worse if intervention is delayed, we may elect an intervention that is quickest to initiate.

(g) The educative or preventative nature of consultation. A primary goal of consultation is to make consultees more effective professionals with particular clients and others. Often an intervention directed at the consultee will help future clients and thus is preferred over others that help only the particular client. Additional factors include: Level of family–school cooperation for interventions where parents must be involved and level of system support from school administrators and common school practices (Briesch, Chafouleas, Neugebauer, & Riley-Tillman, 2013).

Of course the consultant and consultee can choose more than one intervention. It is always useful to have a backup plan B in the form of another intervention to try if the first does not seem to be working.

Guidelines for Generating Interventions

Interpersonal-Behavioral

a) Explore possible interventions to address the client's problems based on best practice and on theory.

b) Determine what interventions have been tried for this client and others with similarly defined problems and why they did or did not work.

c) Admit to uncertainty if that is the case.

d) Foster the experimental attitude by acknowledging the need to evaluate intentions.

e) Prepare a plan B with the consultee if possible.

f) Evaluate evidence supporting intervention strategy.

g) Consider what adaptations to the intervention will be needed to make it culturally appropriate.

Intrapersonal-Cerebral

a) Determine if the problem has been sufficiently defined and analyzed to move to intervention.

b) Determine if the consultee sufficiently vented and gained control over feelings.

c) Review psychological theory that may be applicable to addressing the client's difficulties.

d) Evaluate consultee's readiness to overcome any previous deficiencies including whether theme interference has been eliminated or reduced.

Self-Monitoring Questions

a) What is the most promising intervention of those available?
b) How do particular interventions stand up to the Davis and Sandoval criteria?
c) What biases do I have about particular theories and intervention types?
d) Does the consultee seem ready and able to implement the intervention?

References

Abidin, R.A., Jr. (1975). Negative effects of behavioral consultation: "I know I ought to but it hurts too much." *Journal of School Psychology, 13,* 51–56.

Ainsworth, M.D. (1969). Object relations, dependency, and attachment: A theoretical review of the infant-mother relationship. *Child Development, 40,* 969–1025.

Bergan, J.R., & Kratochwill, T.R. (1990). *Behavioral consultation and therapy.* New York: Plenum.

Blanco, R.F. (1972). *Prescriptions for children with learning and adjustment problems.* Oxford: Charles C. Thomas.

Briesch, A.M., Chafouleas, S.M., Neugebauer, S.R., & Riley-Tillman, C. (2013). Assessing influences on intervention implementation: Revision of the usage rating profile-intervention. *Journal of School Psychology, 51,* 81–96.

Caplan-Moskovich, R. B., & Caplan, G. (2004). Consultee-centered consultation in low feasibility settings. In N. M. Lambert, I. Hylander, & J. Sandoval (Eds.), *Consultee-centered consultation: Improving the quality of professional services in schools and community organizations* (pp. 187–201). Mahwah, NJ: Lawrence Erlbaum.

Cohen, J.J., & Fish, M.C. (1993). *Handbook of school-based interventions.* San Francisco: Jossey-Bass.

Davis, J. M., & Sandoval, J. (1991). A pragmatic framework for systems-oriented consultation. *Journal of Educational and Psychological Consultation, 2,* 201–216.

Elliott, S.N., & Ershier, J. (1990). Best practices in preschool social skills training. In A. Thomas & J. Grimes (Eds.), *Best practices in school psychology—II* (pp. 591–606). Washington, DC: The National Association of School Psychologists.

Elliott, S.N., Witt, J.C., Galvin, G.A., & Peterson, R. (1984). Acceptability of positive and reductive behavioral interventions: Factors that influence teacher's decisions. *Journal of School Psychology, 22,* 353–360.

Gagne, R.M. (1985). *The conditions of learning and theory of instruction.* Belmont, CA: Wadsworth.

Grimes, J. (Ed.). (1982). *Psychological approaches to problems of children and adolescents.* Des Moines, IA: Department of Public Instruction.

Guvå, G., (2004). Meeting a teacher who asks for help, but not for consultation. In N.M. Lambert, I. Hylander, & J.H. Sandoval (Eds.), *Consultee-centered consultation* (pp. 257–266). Mahwah, NJ: Lawrence Erlbaum.

Hylander, I. (2004). Analysis of conceptual change in consultee-centered consultation. In N.M. Lambert, I. Hylander, & J.H. Sandoval (Eds.), *Consultee-centered consultation* (pp. 45–61). Mahwah, NJ: Lawrence Erlbaum.

Ingraham, C.L., & Oka, E.R. (2006). Multicultural issues in evidence-based intervention. *Journal of Applied School Psychology, 22*(2), 127–149.

Millman, H.L., Schaefer, C.E., & Cohen, J.J. (1980). *Therapies for school behavior problems: A handbook of practical interventions.* San Francisco: Jossey-Bass.

Noell, G.H. (2008). Research examining the relationships among consultation process, treatment integrity and outcomes. In W.P. Erchul & S.M. Sheridan (Eds.), *Handbook of research in school consultation: Empirical foundations for the field* (pp. 323–342). New York: Erlbaum/Taylor & Francis.

Odom, S.L., McConnell, S.R., & Chandler, L.K. (1993). Acceptability and feasibility of classroom-based social interaction interventions for young children with disabilities. *Exceptional Children, 60,* 226–236.

Rosenfield, S.A. (1987). *Instructional consultation.* Hillsdale, NJ: Lawrence Erlbaum.

Sanetti, L.M.H., Kratochwill, T.R., & Long, A.C.J. (2013). Applying adult behavior change theory to support mediator-based intervention implementation. *Journal of School Psychology, 28,* 47–62.

Thomas, A., & Grimes, J. (Eds.). (1997) *Best practices in school psychology-V.* Bethesda, MD: National Association of School Psychologists.

Vannest, K.J., Reynolds, C.R., & Kamphaus, R.W. (2008). *BASC-2 intervention guide.* Minneapolis: Pearson.

Witt, J.C. (1986). Teachers' resistance to the use of school-based interventions. *Journal of School Psychology, 24,* 37–44.

Witt, J.C., & Elliott, S.N. (1985). Acceptability of classroom management strategies. In T.R. Kratochwll (Ed.), *Advances in school psychology* (Vol. 4, pp. 251–288). Hillsdale, NJ: Erlbaum.

9
SUPPORTING INTERVENTION AND EXPERIMENTATION

The title of this chapter contains the terms experimentation and intervention. In the consultation literature and elsewhere the term intervention denotes a strategic change made in the way the consultee treats the client or the client's environment. Ideally the change is based on theory and has been empirically validated, albeit tested in settings that are likely different in some respect from where it is being currently implemented. As a result, interventions are relatively prescriptive in that there is a protocol, and there is a demonstrated likelihood of success.

The term experiment implies the testing of a hypothesis where the design permits the hypothesis to either be supported or not. The outcome of an experiment is unknown and the result may result in either a desired effect or a failure (i.e., no change or no difference). In consultation, even when the consultee is making a change based on a strategy with demonstrated effectiveness, it is useful to treat the intervention as an experiment. Supporting the consultee in making changes involves fostering the experimental attitude.

The experimental attitude has several components. First, before beginning a change, there is the acknowledgement of the possibility of failure. Human problems are difficult to solve. A process is needed to solve problems that may involve some trial and error. Second, often there is much information to be gained from failure. It is possible to reflect on the assumptions that went into an unsuccessful attempt and to review how procedures were implemented with an intention to understand what went wrong. Third, most inventors tell us that persistence pays off, and trying multiple strategies is usually called for, suggesting that intervention is a continuing process, not a magic trick. Fourth, there is a need to evaluate outcomes at multiple points across time. It is important to acknowledge that success may not be lasting and that new, different problems may emerge. There will be a continuing need for support. Intervention may proceed in a step-by-step manner over time.

Framing consultation as experimental and the consultee as an investigator is one way to help the consultee continue to be motivated to work on the problem. However, the consultant also helps assure the success of consultation (a) by determining that the proposals identified to address the consultation problem continue to be acceptable to the consultee, (b) by attending to how faithful the consultee is to the plan, (c) by providing formative evaluation, and (d) by providing emotional support.

Revisiting Treatment Acceptability

In the last chapter there was mention of treatment acceptability as one of the ways to choose among multiple interventions. Treatment acceptability, also termed *social validity*, refers to the consultee's evaluation of a proposed intervention. It is considered during the intervention generation process but may be revisited during or after an intervention trial, particularly if the consultee has been reluctant.

Consultants and consultees may first ask, "Is the intervention acceptable philosophically?" Teachers are often concerned about issues of fairness, for example. They often believe that to be fair, no child should receive more attention or privileges than another. They may be uncomfortable in devoting more attention to one child than another. The consultant can help the consultee in coming to appreciate that fairness also means addressing each child's needs and that these needs differ. Discussion can help resolve this issue for the consultee.

Teachers also tend to favor interventions that are positive rather than negative in tone. They prefer to be perceived as nice and helpful by the child rather than as punishing or mean. Helping teachers understand the need for structure and limits in the classroom and their role as adults rather than peers may help them act differently with a pupil.

As the intervention begins to be implemented, the consultant may ask, "Does the intervention make sense?" and "Has the consultee, after the passage of time, continued to view the intervention as understandable and appropriate?" Occasionally consultees will agree to a strategy during consultation only to become confused later. A follow-up with the consultee to determine their understanding of the intervention may be necessary. Overly complex interventions and those that seem counterintuitive will be particularly vulnerable to second thoughts. The consultant must keep ideas as simple as possible.

All interventions must be adapted to the setting in which they are to be implemented. A highly effective intervention may have been developed and validated in middle-class schools with extraordinary resources. To implement it in an inner city school with minimal resources and a population living in poverty will take some creativity. The consultant should ask, "Does the intervention seem doable in the consultee's setting?" or "Has the intervention been adapted properly to this setting?" It may seem like the intervention is feasible initially, but in the process of putting it in place in the classroom or school the consultee and consultant may discover unanticipated barriers that will require rethinking. This point will be expanded in the next chapter as a particular problem in multicultural settings.

One factor that is important in treatment acceptability is whether the consultee believes the intervention will work in his or her classroom. The consultant must consider, "Does the consultee still see the intervention as having a high probability of success?" Behavior may be slow in changing and if new or different limits are set on the client, there is likely to be testing of those limits. The consultee may become discouraged and begin to doubt the likelihood of success. The consultant must be prepared to give realistic encouragement as appropriate.

In making changes in a system such as the classroom we can almost always expect there to be some unanticipated outcomes. The system has adapted to current circumstances and the drive toward homeostasis leads to resistance to change. With a change in the client's behavior, the client's role in the classroom will likely change. Other children in the classroom may take the client's place, for example, by becoming the class scapegoat or clown. In addition, changes in procedure or rules may cause difficulties in managing other students. As they arise, the consultant must be available to discuss and reflect with the consultee what can be done to ameliorate unanticipated outcomes that have arisen. A need to additionally address the needs of others of the consultee's clients may be necessary.

Sanetti, Kratochwill, and Long (2013) pointed out that supporting the consultee's intention to implement a strategy, and his or her sense of self-efficacy, leads to continued persistence in implementing a plan. Some support strategies are modeling behavior, role play, and continued consultation dialogue.

Treatment acceptability is perhaps necessary but not sufficient for determining how well the consultee follows through and implements an intervention correctly or as designed and validated elsewhere. A willingness to try a new approach does not mean that the new approach will be done well. The consultant and consultee must evaluate the execution of the intervention.

Evaluating Treatment Integrity

The issue of treatment integrity or treatment fidelity has been studied and researched extensively, particularly by psychologists coming from a behavioral tradition. Typically for any intervention or strategy, psychologists have developed a protocol for how it is to be delivered. The protocol includes a step-by-step set of consultee behaviors and responses to client behaviors that have been shown to be effective in bringing about change. The protocol may also specify materials, timing, context, or other things that must be in place for the intervention to work. This protocol has typically been validated in a research setting. The question becomes, can the consultee follow this protocol?

Noell (2008) distinguishes between two kinds of treatment integrity in consultation: treatment plan implementation integrity and consultation procedural integrity. The latter refers to the degree to which the consultant adheres to an established consultation model and the degree to which specific procedures embedded within an established consultation model are implemented as designed. A later section will address an examination of the consultation process.

An examination of treatment plan implementation integrity starts with the question, "Has the consultee been able to implement the intervention with fidelity?" Follow-up questions are "Did the consultee understand it?"; "Did they have the skill, self-confidence, and perspective to implement it as validated?"; "Has it been modified appropriately for the setting in which it was to be used?"; and "Has enough time elapsed or trials been completed for an effect to be measured?"

Data are needed to answer these questions. If an explicit protocol for an intervention exists, the consultee, the consultant, or a third party can use it as a guide for observation or reflection. Often consultants make a checklist available. The consultee can self-report on the extent to which the protocol was adhered to, or the consultant and consultee can review and discuss recordings of what transpired. Additionally, if the client's behavior has been recorded, these data can be used to determine how things have gone. The consultant may elect to be present when a consultee introduces as a new innovation in the classroom both to demonstrate commitment and support and to provide immediate feedback in the spirit of formative evaluation.

If treatment integrity has been verified and the client has not made significant improvement, it seems reasonable to believe that a new conceptualization may be in order. This implies returning to an earlier stage in the process and considering a new hypothesis, using the intervention failure as additional information.

Formative Evaluation

Evaluators make the distinction between formative and summative evaluation. Formative evaluation involves collecting information throughout the implementation of a program and using that information to modify or correct the implementation to assure a successful outcome. Summative evaluation consists of collecting data at the conclusion of a program to determine if the program is successful and is cost effective. The next chapter discusses summative evaluation in consultation. To support consultees in making changes, concepts from formative evaluation have relevance.

Formative evaluation works by collecting data on how the program is working and feeding it back to a program director (consultee). It looks for progress in meeting established milestones and notes problems and unanticipated difficulties. By delivering the information in a timely manner, the program director can make changes in the protocol being used. If data on a child's target behavior are being collected, as recommended by behavioral consultants, this information will form the basis of important feedback. Seeing changes over time in concrete terms, such as displayed on a graph, is important in maintaining motivation to continue and has been shown to increase treatment integrity (Noell, 2008). Noell argued that the absence of objective data decreases treatment plan implementation, and that data-based feedback may be more important than extensive prior training in the intervention. The consultant can join with the consultee as they examine and interpret formative evaluation information.

Offering Emotional Support

For the consultee, making changes in their professional behavior often involves taking a risk with the attendant anxiety. Consultants must deal with lack of self-confidence as it arises during the intervention stage.

One important principle is to avoid giving false reassurance. The consultant can be encouraging but must also acknowledge that the intervention may not work with this client. Encouragement may take the form of praising small successes and the consultee's willingness to tackle a difficult problem. However, an additional message to the consultee is that it is not the end of the world if the intervention does not work. The consultant will be not disturbed by an initial failure and will be available to continue collaborating on the problem. There must be the right balance between supporting the consultee's efforts and reducing the stakes or consequences of lack of success.

As at other points in consultation, nonverbal ways of supporting the consultee are important. The consultant continues to listen attentively to the consultee, but does not mirror any feelings of distress. The consultant maintains a relaxed stance, keeps relatively neutral facial expressions, and otherwise communicates nonjudgmental acceptance of the consultee.

When failure is encountered, Berlin (1977) argues that the consultant must be ready "to illustrate from his own experience that he, too, has on occasions failed to be helpful [with a client] . . . It seems to be helpful to the teacher when the consultant comments that one can fail with a clear conscience after one has literally done everything one can within his own present scope of knowledge and professional development" (p. 33). The consultant relates past professional failures objectively and reflects on them seriously, acknowledging that everyone has limitations. This kind of consultant self-disclosure, Berlin suggested, frees both the consultant and consultee to try again.

If consonant with the consultant's personality, the appropriate uses of humor may also facilitate coping on the part of the consultee. Humor and irony often enables us to take a different perspective on a situation and to release built up tension.

Besides the consultant, peers may also supply emotional support in many of the same ways. They are able to share similar feelings and frustrations, and also advice on how they have dealt with analogous problems or implemented the strategy in question. This is one of the advantages of group consultation, a topic covered in a later chapter.

A final way to support the consultee is to use some of the techniques associated with solution-oriented counseling and consultation. The solution-oriented approach involves getting the consultee to focus on the future rather than the past, and to envision positive outcomes for the client (Brown, Pryzwansky, & Schulte, 2011). Key assumptions and applications are:

1. When the consultee has the opportunity to imagine how things will be different when an intervention is implemented, they will view the intervention protocol as more realizable and be willing to invest in it. Following this idea, the consultant may continue to bring up the goal of the intervention and how the relationship with the client would be improved.
2. When consultees explore when things worked well with the intervention, they will be more likely to be motivated and more confident in their own resources and abilities. Again this idea implies that the consultant should help the consultee be alert to success and acknowledge it, even though improvements may be slight.
3. The strategic use of presuppositional questions will help motivate the consultee. Presuppositional questions are questions that stimulate the consultee to respond in ways that are self-enhancing and strength-promoting. Typically they imply that change is inevitable and that new perspectives have merit. Some examples of presuppositional questions are, "What have you changed in your classroom this week that worked?"; "What have you learned from trying this new way of behaving?"; and "Have you come to see any evidence that our latest hypothesis has merit?"

Consultation Process Integrity

Another way support interventions and experiments is to be sure that the consultation process has gone as planned. This determination requires the consultant to reflect on what has happened to date and to make corrections that will enable creative thinking in the consultant and consultee. Defining consultation process integrity, Noell (2008) asks the question, "Does the consultation assessment and analysis model identify an intervention that has a high probability of success?" The consultee-centered consultant would ask instead, "Has consultation proceeded to the point where the professional relationship between the consultee and client (the teacher and child) has been restored and improved?" One way to structure this evaluation is for the consultant to answer the questions listed at the end of Chapters 3 through 10.

Rescuing Consultee-Centered Consultation

Hylander (2004, 2012) has identified a number of situations where the consultation process gets derailed or comes to a halt. She called these *blind alleys*. Through formative evaluation of the consultation process she believed it is possible for the consultant to recognize when the consultation process starts to get into trouble and to get it back on track. She argued that consultation bogs down when the consultant is inflexible and unwilling to change his or her own conceptualization of the issue, or his or her way of interacting with the consultee. An indicator of entering a blind alley is the consultant feeling overwhelmed by negative feelings, either before or after the session. There are three major forms of blind alleys, each associates with one mode of interaction or phase of consultation called *binds*, *boredom*, and *break-ups*. Each has subtypes defined by the relationship between the consultant's and consultee's conceptualizations and how they express them.

Binds during the Approach Mode

Binds in consultation occur when the consultant and consultee both seem to agree on the problem. Here the consultant uses active listening and finds it easy to validate what the consultee says and seems to understand about the problem. The consultant has no problem summarizing the consultee's position, and the consultee is able to discharge feelings, but nothing changes. If the consultant asks speculative questions or makes challenging comments, the consultee objects. The problem stems from the consultant not recognizing or not acting on the fact that the consultee's verbal presentation does not match the consultee's conceptual representation. For some reason the consultee is not able to present her true thoughts to the consultant. Often this is because the consultee is overly emotionally involved with the client, and cannot admit worry or anger. Hylander has identified three binds.

The Nice Party

In the nice party, the consultant and consultee share verbal presentations and cognitive representations (which do not match), but the consultant does not introduce his or her conceptualization of the situation, even though it agrees with the consultee's hidden conceptualization, for fear of being perceived as critical. The consultation remains in the nondirective mode with the consultant confirming the consultee's presentation. The consultation conversation remains pleasant and friendly and the consultant believes the process is going very well. The consultee discharges feelings and is happy to have his or her impressions and behaviors validated but does not listen to neutral questions and strongly objects to challenges. There is an elephant in the room that does not get discussed. This may result in a *false turning* when the consultee says the issue is resolved. Because it has been a nice party, the consultee will want to please the consultant by reporting changes.

Walking in Mud

The difference between *walking in mud* and being stuck *in a nice party* is the affect of the consultant, and the fact that the consultant comes to adopt the consultee's presentation as the consultee's real representation. The label *walking in mud* reflects how the consultant feels: heavy, encumbered, and hopeless. This situation is often the result of identifying with the consultee and the consultee's depiction of the dilemma. The consultant accepts what the consultee has presented as a valid cognitive representation of the problem even though the consultee, in fact, holds a different hidden idea. The consultant has been seduced by the presentation and has not questioned it sufficiently. As the consultant continues to attend to the consultee's presentation without challenge, there will be more details supporting the presented position. The only way out of this dead end is for the consultant to continually challenge his or her own theories of what is happening. With luck the consultant will hit on the hidden representation of the consultee and will introduce it into the dialogue. If this happens, the consultee may be able to move forward.

The Hidden Fight

A hidden fight occurs when the consultant's cognitive representation is very different from the consultee's. Again, the consultant is reluctant to introduce his or her theory of the dilemma directly for fear of alienating the consultee. The consultant holds onto the cognitive representation, however, and continues to attempt ways to introduce it into the conversation. At the same time, the consultee persists in maintaining his or her original cognitive representation. The only way out of this alley is if the consultant gives up his or her original conceptualization and moves on to a different one in the hope it will provoke change.

Boredom during the Free Association Mode

Consultation can also end up in a blind alley during the free association mode. Boredom ensues when the consultee presents a problem in a way consistent with his or her cognitive representation. The consultant, however, has the same cognitive representation and thus the presentations of the problem are similar. Since this cognitive representation has not been fruitful in showing the way to a possible intervention, unless the consultant can entertain a new representation, the consultation will go nowhere. However if the conversation continues and new data are collected and the consultant is aware of it, the consultant may form a new representation. By identifying a new way of understanding and framing the dilemma and introducing it, it is possible the consultation may emerge from the dead end.

Break during the Moving Away Mode

Consultation may breakdown at the point when there is an attempt to form a new conceptualization of the consultation dilemma. If the consultant and consultee have radically different ideas about the causes and solution for the problem, and the consultant has challenged the consultee's conceptualization too vigorously, the consultee may respond by changing his or her verbal presentation of the problem away from the consultant's verbal explanation. Eventually the consultee may terminate the consultation and seek other remedies such as a special education placement. The consultant has challenged the consultee too much, while not challenging his or her own conception of the problem.

Hylander (2004) described three types of breakdowns.

Tug of War

A tug of war occurs when both the consultant and consultee attempt to impose their differing cognitive representations on each other by continually presenting theory and defending its correctness. A breakdown at this point is common. "This is common when a consultee wants to refer a child somewhere else or get an extra aid to take care of the problem. It may also be the case when teachers are convinced that a child has a special kind of diagnosis, which the consultant does not agree to" (Hylander, 2004, p. 56). The consultant must be flexible in shifting either their representation of the problem or their presentation.

Interpretative Relation

An interpretive relationship occurs when the consultant responds directly to what he or she believes is the consultee's representation of the problem and ignores the consultee's presentation. In addition the consultant makes this interpretation his or her own presentation rather than attending to the consultee's presentation first. The consultant does not consider the presentation but intuits the representation directly. Often the consultee will object if the interpretation is premature, coming before the consultant responds to the presentation. If the consultant persists with interpretation before the consultee is ready and is not flexible, a breakdown may occur.

Mission Impossible

A mission impossible situation may occur when, in spite of the fact that the consultant's cognitive representation is close to the consultee's verbal presentation and cognitive representation, the consultant makes a contrary presentation. Hylander (2004) offers the example of "a consultee who believes that a child has severe psychiatric difficulties and needs something else than what they have to offer. The consultant actually agrees, believing that what the consultees do and could do is not enough but still insists in discussing how they could relate to the child and keep him in the group. In this case the only thing the consultant can do is give up her presentation, or change her own representation" (p. 58). In this case, the consultant is not being true to his or her own representation and is presenting inconsistent ideas.

Hylander found that consultants in her study were very good at avoiding blind alleys. However many consultants found that if they were able to extricate themselves from a blind alley, consultation could continue with dramatic results. The key to moving forward is for the consultant to challenge his or her own initial cognitive representation of the problem and how to respond to it. She states, "Consultant flexibility of representation is a key to consultation and conceptual change" (Hylander, 2004, p. 59).

Guidelines for Supporting Intervention and Experimentation

Interpersonal-Behavioral

a) Promote the experimental attitude by stressing the need for data and the possibility of failure.
b) Check to see how well treatment is being implemented.
c) Check to see if the treatment has been modified appropriately for the setting and client.
d) Collect formative evaluation data and discuss with consultee.
e) Support the consultee through difficult times. Share personal experiences of failure and frustration and provide support though nonverbal behavior.

Intrapersonal-Cerebral

a) Determine if treatment continues to be acceptable to the consultee.
b) Determine the consultee's need for emotional support.
c) Assess whether the intervention was implemented with integrity.

Self-Monitoring Questions

a) Have I helped the consultee understand the intervention?
b) Have I offered enough emotional support to the consultee so that he or she will implement the intervention with fidelity?
c) Have I addressed any lacks of skill, self-confidence, or perspective to allow the consultee to to implement the intervention as validated?
d) Is the consultee cooperating with me just to please me or humor me?
e) Has consultation proceeded to the point where the professional relationship between the consultee and client has been restored and improved or will I have to continue to offer support?
f) Have I avoided binds, boredom, and breaks by being flexible in considering different representations of the problem?

References

Berlin, I. N. (1977). Some lessons learned in 25 years of mental health consultation to schools. In S.C. Plog & P.I. Ahmed (Eds.), *Principles and techniques of mental health consultation* (pp. 23–48). New York: Plenum Publishing Corporation.

Brown, D., Pryzwansky, W. B., & Schulte, A. C. (2011). *Psychological consultation and collaboration*. Upper Saddle River, NJ: Pearson.

Davis, J. M., & Sandoval, J. (1991). A pragmatic framework for systems-oriented consultation. *Journal of Educational and Psychological Consultation, 2,* 201–216.

Fullan, M. (1996). Professional culture and educational change. *School Psychology Review, 25,* 496–500.

Hylander, I. (2004). Analysis of conceptual change in consutee-centered consultation. In N. M. Lambert, I. Hylander, & J. H. Sandoval (Eds.), *Consultee-centered consultation* (pp. 45–61). Mahwah, NJ: Lawrence Erlbaum.

Hylander, I. (2012). Conceptual change through consultee-centered consultation: A theoretical model. *Consulting Psychology Journal: Practice and Research, 64,* 29–45.

Idol, L., Paolucci-Whitcomb, P., & Nevin, A. (1986). *Collaborative consultation*. Rockville, MD: Aspen Publications.

Lambert, N.M., Yandell, W., & Sandoval, J.H. (1975). Preparation of school psychologists for school-based consultation: A training activity and a service to community schools. *Journal of School Psychology, 13,* 68–75.

Noell, G.H. (2008). Research examining the relationships among consultation process, treatment integrity, and outcomes. In W.P. Erchul & S.M. Sheridan (Eds.), *Handbook of research in school consultation* (pp. 323–341). New York: Erlbaum/ Taylor & Francis.

O'Hanlon, W.H., & Weiner-Davis, M. (1989). *In search of solutions: A new direction in psychotherapy.* New York: W.W. Norton.

Sandoval, J. (1977). Mental health consultation for teachers in preservice training. *California Journal of Teacher Education, 3,* 110–124.

Sandoval, J. (1996). Constructivism, consultee-centered consultation and conceptual change. *Journal of Educational and Psychological Consultation, 7,* 89–97.

Sanetti, L.M.H., Kratochwill, T.R., & Long, A.C.J. (2013). Applying adult behavior change theory to support mediator-based intervention implementation. *Journal of School Psychology, 28,* 47–62.

Sarason, S.B. (1996). *Revisiting "The culture of the school and the problem of change."* New York: Teachers College Press.

Sheridan, S.M. (1992). Consultant and client outcomes of competency-based behavioral consultation training. *School Psychology Quarterly, 7,* 245–270.

Wilcox, M.R. (1980). Variables affecting group mental health consultation for teachers. *Professional Psychology, 11,* 728–732.

Zins, J.E., Kratochwill, T.R., & Elliott, S.N. (Eds.). (1993). *Handbook of consultation services for children: Applications in educational and clinical settings.* San Francisco: Jossey-Bass.

10

FOLLOW-UP AND DISENGAGEMENT

Experience suggests that the consultation process takes place over three to four sessions on a particular case, although difficult cases will require more meetings. The final session will occur when there has been time for the consultee to implement changes with the client and sufficient time has passed to evaluate the impact of those changes. The primary outcome we are looking for is an improvement in the working relationship with the client. Such improvement suggests that the client is functioning more effectively in school.

In the last session the task is to do follow-up and then either to return to an earlier phase of problem solving or to disengage from the case. At this point in the consultation relationship, the consultant and consultee agree that either (a) the presented problem has been satisfactorily dealt with, (b) further information or intervention is necessary and the work will continue, or (c) there has not been improvement and consultation alone is not sufficient to help the consultee or client. If either outcome (a) or outcome (c) has occurred, the next step is disengagement. Otherwise consultation continues with a return to problem defining and reframing (outcome b). If the consultation dilemma has been resolved and no other issues are present, the disengagement is tentative and a celebration is in order. If the decision is that consultation has not worked, and there is no reason to continue, final termination must be considered. In this chapter we will examine first the follow-up process and then consider disengagement and termination procedures.

Debriefing

The first step in the follow-up process is debriefing. The purpose of the debriefing conversation is finding out what happened in the interim since the last session and evaluating events with the consultee. An additional goal is expressing both the positive and negative feelings that may come up. The consultant usually initiates debriefing by simply asking about what has occurred and how the client is functioning. As the conversation continues, more and more responsibility for evaluation devolves to the consultee.

It is important to schedule time for debriefing. Sufficient time should be set aside to explore fully what has happened. A short, chance encounter with the consultee will not be enough, and instead a formal meeting with sufficient time will be required.

In addition to setting aside time, it is important to prepare in advance any data that will be used in evaluating the outcome of the intervention. Gathering information together and putting it in a usable form, such as graphs or displays of work samples, takes time.

It is also useful to prepare a series of questions to use. Some standard ones are listed in Table 10.1.

The consultant must also be prepared to offer emotional support during debriefing. Success and failure are at the extremes, but many outcomes will be somewhere in between, at least at the time of debriefing. Because the client or the relationship may only have improved slightly, the consultant must be prepared to dispel any consultee irrational beliefs. The consultant should counter negative feelings attached to overly high expectations and perfectionism by pointing out positive aspects or changes, no matter how small, and by reminding the consultee that every person has limitations and that understanding and accepting them is important.

At the same time it may be helpful to temper success. The consultee should celebrate positive feelings of success, but the consultant should point out that

TABLE 10.1 Sample debriefing questions.

1. How comfortable were you in making changes in your classroom (implementing the intervention)?
2. What is the evidence it worked or did not work?
3. What part seemed to work well?
4. What part did not go so well?
5. How could the future use of this intervention be improved?
6. What was the impact on other students?
7. How has your relationship with the client changed?
8. How have you, or should you have, adapted this intervention to the cultural background of the client?
9. Could this intervention be used with other clients?
10. Do you have any suggestions about school policy changes as a result of using this intervention?
11. To what extent have we met our goal?
12. Where shall we go from here?

sometimes children regress under stress. It is well known that maladaptive behaviors can spontaneously recover after a period of time and that new behaviors have to be monitored and supported using an appropriate schedule of reinforcement. In addition, new problems may emerge if the client's previous motivation has only been temporarily diverted.

Facilitating Transfer

A second step in the follow-up process is the facilitation of transfer. Transfer is an important goal of consultation, a goal that links consultation to prevention. The intention is for the consultee to use a new way of looking at future clients and responding to them in the classroom. Scholars distinguish between *high-road* versus *low-road* transfer (Mayer & Wittrock, 1996; Salomon & Perkins, 1989). The first, high road, are instances of transfer where active retrieval, mapping, and inference processes take place. It requires deliberate reflective processing. In contrast, low-road transfer occurs rather spontaneously and involves automatic processing.

Low-road transfer uses frequently employed mental representations and automated, proceduralized knowledge, and occurs preferably in near-transfer settings, close to the setting where the behavior was learned. For example, once a teacher has mastered a new technique with a child, he or she will continue to use it without thinking about it. In contrast, high-road transfer involves applying new learning to dissimilar settings and clients. This form of transfer is more conception-driven, and requires cognitive and meta-cognitive effort. Perkins and Salomon (2012) posited that it involves detecting a potential relationship with prior leaning, electing to pursue it, and working out a fruitful connection. To facilitate high-road transfer the consultant can explicitly bring up extensions and applications of any new consultee conceptualizations. Some examples of consultation questions and leads are:

> Are there other kids who could benefit from this way of working?
> Do you see this pattern/explanation of behavior in other children?
> Do you remember other children for whom this way of thinking would have helped?

Evaluating Outcomes

At least two types of outcomes are possible: an evaluation of the consultation process itself and an evaluation of the intervention and relationship between the consultee and client. Current evaluation theory stresses the need to involve the recipient of a program in the process of evaluation. New directions in evaluating consultee-centered consultation would suggest an early partnership between the consultee and the consultant in planning and executing the evaluation process, possibly in the first session as they discuss the problem. A question the consultant might pose to the consultee is "How will we know when this process has been helpful?" Follow-up questions (which the consultant would also try to answer for him or herself, in the spirit of brainstorming) would include "How will you feel differently if we are successful?" or "How might your understanding of the problem and possible interventions change?"

Two general types of evaluation data are changes in the client and changes in the consultee. Many theorists focus exclusively on changes in the client as the most important of the two types, and ignore or minimize changes in the consultee. Purists from the behavioral tradition, for example, would even limit evaluation to an examination of changes in specific observable behavior of the client. These changes in target behaviors, determined in the early stages of consultation, are the primary, or the only, types of evaluation data deemed useful.

Although changes in behavior are important and informative, consultee-centered consultants argue that changes in conceptualizations or representations, which are not directly observable, are also critical criteria to use in determining consultation effectiveness. Conceptualizations are broad understandings of phenomena and of the network of associations individuals have to them (some of which may be affectively loaded). Changes may occur in the consultee's understanding of the problem, or of the client, or of her or himself. Changes may also occur in the understanding of the process of consultation. Changes in consultee conceptualizations are certainly more accessible than changes in client conceptualizations. Finally, in consultee-centered consultation it is also important to examine changes in affect in the consultee. A goal is to reduce anxiety and anger or depression. Reduction in anxiety or other negative affect is an important source of information or indicator about how consultation is working.

Changes in Client Behavior

Traditional evaluation focuses on identifying behaviors in the client that are causing difficulty for the consultee and then documenting changes in these behaviors following interventions generated during consultation. This strategy makes sense to the extent that the behaviors are real and are the central issues in the consultation predicament. Consultation may be effective, particularly in reducing the consultee's lack of confidence, when it changes the way the behavior is framed by the consultee. Consequently, consultation may be effective even when observable behavior does not change or changes subtly. Nevertheless, change in client behavior remains an important outcome to evaluate and is a key to accountability.

Although changes in the client have been traditionally considered as the goal of evaluation in most forms of consultation, in consultee-centered consultation it is also important to examine the effect of consultation on a whole range of clients worked with by the consultee, as well as the identified client. One central premise is that consultation will result in improved performance of the consultee in working with other clients. This improvement occurs because consultation interventions work to bring about changes in consultee perceptions and attitudes and then, in turn, change in consultee-client behavior and, finally, a change in client behavior and performance. We are hoping for what Gagne (1985) calls horizontal transfer of learning. He noted that this form of transfer is often difficult to bring about.

Unless the consultant spends a great deal of time in the school serving the client, there is little chance to observe first-hand changes in the client or other similar clients. These changes can be observed by supervisors or may be reflected in data routinely collected by the institution such as attendance data, achievement data, or disciplinary actions or referrals for other assistance. The consultee will also be able to report changes in the client, but the consultee must be considered a biased source of information. As mentioned in Chapter 5, there are observational technologies available to record the frequency and intensity of target behaviors and to chart changes over time. If the consultee is willing to collect this information and it is feasible to do so in the situation, observational data will produce more objective information. Others in the consultee's system, such as assistants or other clients, can be taught to record client behavior in a systematic manner. Information about changes in the client must be cross-validated using more than one source, however.

Changes in Consultee Behavior

Changes in consultee behavior and performance can be noted by the consultee, the consultant, the consultee's supervisors and peers, and the clients. Each of these sources can contribute useful information, but each has its drawbacks.

The consultant can usually only indirectly judge changes in behavior. Changes in behavior that are reported by the consultee are difficult to evaluate because they may be influenced by conscious or unconscious motivation. Caplan (1970) pointed out some of the problems of consultee self-report: "Moreover, a consultee's report to his consultant about changes in his behavior with a client must be accepted with some caution, since it will often be colored by the consultee's awareness of what he thinks the consultant would like to hear and by the complexities of the consultee-consultant relationship. A consultee may reward or punish his consultant by such a report" (p. 296). Nevertheless self-reports are one source of information.

In addition to self-reports on the part of consultees, the consultant can observe the consultation process. To permit the observation of change, the consultant must keep a careful record of the consultation process. Using notes collected during or after each session, the consultant keeps track of the problem or predicament discussed, the thread of the discussion, the consultation strategies or approaches used, the consultee's emotional responses, and the consultant's thoughts and feelings. In addition, after the session, the consultant should record the result of his or her reflections on the session. These notes can be used as one source of evaluative information, about the consultant as well as the consultee.

The consultant can examine shifts in the sort of referrals or types of problems brought to consultation by the consultee. If the same predicaments or types of clients continue to show up in consultation, it may be a sign that positive transfer is not occurring. One may be misled, moreover, if there is a reduction in the number of clients brought to consultation over time. This reduction may represent transfer, but may also represent increased *comfort* with clients with a particular behavior, but not necessarily increased *competence* in meeting the needs of these clients. In addition, a reduction may also indicate that the consultant is not perceived to be of help with this sort of case. Nevertheless, coupled with other evidence, a reduction in the number and type of referrals would generally be a sign that consultation is working.

Since the goal is change in behavior with respect to new clients with similar profiles, a comprehensive evaluation will need to extend over some time in order to determine if the desired outcomes occur with new clients. As a result it is useful to build in long-term follow-ups, either by questionnaire or interview, to get an accurate picture of success.

The consultee's supervisors and colleagues may also provide information about behavior change and increased competency if asked. As Caplan (1970) pointed out, these reports may also be biased. Indirect evidence, such as increased requests from administrators for consultation services, may support observations of improvement in the job performance of consultees. The consultant, because of different professional training, may or may not be able to tell if changes in performance are for the better or worse, but peers and supervisors from the peers' profession can note changes and evaluate them. Changes in behavior may be noted on routine performance evaluations collected by the consultee's organization. Alternatively, the consultant and consultee may design questions and probes designed to identify changes in behavior.

Clients, too, can be brought into the evaluation process, although often this will be awkward. In some situations, such as high school and college teaching, there have been attempts to get information from clients or client's peers about professionals. These evaluations may be examined to detect changes in performance following consultation.

Changes in Consultee Attitude and Affect

The consultant can also observe changes in consultee attitude. Attitude change is often revealed in both verbal and nonverbal behaviors. Traditional signs of reduced anxiety that can be observed are relaxed body language and appearance, improved sense of humor, and a reduction in the level of confusion and distractibility. In addition, the consultant can note the gradual shift in anxiety across clients with similar features, as the consultee's capacity to cope improves.

The consultee, too, can be a source of information. The consultant can ask about changes in attitude and affect, but, as with other self-reports, the responses will need cross-validation. Talking about problems with a skilled and empathetic listener typically brings about a reduction in tension. If consultation is effective, however, this relief will not be temporary, but lasting. The consultant should expect a gradual increase in signs of coping on the part of the consultee. If the consultee returns week after week at the same level of agitation, there is evidence that new strategies must be employed.

Consultee self-reports and consultee satisfaction or the reduction in anxiety about the consultation issue are legitimate factors to evaluate and document. In developing a protocol for evaluating consultee satisfaction it is important to consider all possibilities: lack of knowledge, lack of skill, lack of self-confidence, and lack of objectivity. Items must be developed to tap each of these domains. The literature contains many examples (Sandoval, 2004).

Clients might also be a source of information about changes in consultee attitudes and understandings. To the extent that clients react to the climate established by the consultee, they may also reflect the disposition of the consultee. They may be observed to be more relaxed and comfortable with the consultee, quite apart from changing their behavior, as a result of a successful consultation. In general, the consultee will need to be the major source of information about changes in conceptualization.

Evaluating the Consultant

Information from evaluation is important to identify professional strengths and weaknesses on the part of the consultant. Responsible consultants continue to engage in reflective practice (Garcia, 2004) aimed at improving their personal development as consultants and take time to collect information and review their professional practices. Simple reflection, with or without the aid of a peer, can be thought of as part of the consultation evaluation process. But reflection alone is not sufficient. There is a danger that reflection in the absence of data from other sources can become self-serving and self-deluding and subject to a number of cognitive biases. Reflection combined with multisource data can lead to improved service, however.

It also may be important to examine changes in the behavior, conceptualizations, and affect in the *consultant*. The consultant finding it easy to cancel consultations or arriving late, the consultant forming negative attitudes about consultees or clients, and the consultant feeling anxious or bored during consultation has data at hand that things are not going well. Reflection and peer review should look at what is occurring in the consultant's behavior and thoughts as well as changes in the consultee and client. In addition to self-examination on the part of the consultant, several measures of consultee satisfaction with consultation have been developed (e.g., Conoley & Conoley, 1982; Gallessich, 1982; Parsons & Meyers, 1984). These measures include reports of consultant behavior that provide important feedback.

Disengagement and Termination Disengagement

The consultee and consultant may disengage when the consultee or consultant no longer feels the need. Since consultation is voluntary, the consultee may choose not to continue at any time. It is important, however, for the consultant to probe the reason for the wish not to continue. The consultant may ask "what has changed?" and whether the consultee is sure the dilemma has been solved. Ideally, the dilemma is resolved and there are clear indicators! Sometimes there is what Hylander called a magic turning after the first session, and no further work will be needed. Simply talking about the problem with an empathetic professional may discharge emotional impediments to a successful working relationship between the client and consultee, or the consultee may have been able to come to a new conceptualization of the client on his or her own.

Timing of Disengagement

Consultation in schools is somewhat different from other settings in that the school-based mental health professional consultant will continue to be available during the school year (and often for multiple years, if their assignment does not change). Disengagement can occur at any time when the relationship with the client has been restored and the consultee has gained knowledge, skill, self-confidence, and objectivity.

But consultation can also end because of naturally occurring events. At the end of the school year, most consultees will say goodbye to their clients, whether or not a dilemma has been solved. In addition, student clients may transfer to another school or program. Even if a particular client is no longer in the picture, the consultant and consultee will still be able to continue with new clients and dilemmas.

Consultation is often ongoing in the school setting and, if the relationship has been rewarding to the participants, the consultees will bring up new dilemmas with different clients. This can occur immediately or after some time has passed. In this case, disengagement is "soft," because it is not the end of a relationship. However, consultants should be on guard against dependency on the part of the consultee and not be seduced into continuing a relationship for its own sake. It is pleasant to spend time talking about work, particularly when teachers or administrators have few adults to talk to. Ideally, in time and as the consultee gains competence, the number of dilemmas brought to consultation will decline and the time between requests for consultation will increase as independence is achieved.

It is also true that consultation can go on too long and the consultant must look for signs that his or her help is no longer needed. Berlin (1966) gives an example: "I began to notice that I was not only enjoying the meetings, that the mutual regard was stimulating and pleasurable, but also that the meetings had become less serious and less work-oriented. There were more playful exchanges, more time was devoted to casual talk and less time to problem solving. The problems that were brought for discussion were not very serious ones" (p. 179). At this point the consultant can move toward disengagement, emphasizing that he or she will still be available if needed.

Disengagement Process

The process of disengagement includes taking time to look back on the process and what is new that has been learned. The consultant may ask, "what have we learned about this client and ourselves?" A brief summary of what has occurred is appropriate.

An important part of disengagement is to celebrate successes. The consultant should congratulate the consultee on their new working relationship with the client and also provide positive nonverbal acknowledgement, such as smiles, a "high five," or a handshake.

The consultant might also be sure that the consultee is aware of how he or she may get back in touch with the consultant. There might be plans for a long-term follow-up on the client, or at least a request to do so. The consultee may also be encouraged to find other sources of support and ideas among peers and supervisors. One such form of support is group consultation, which is the subject of the next chapter.

Termination

It becomes necessary to terminate consultation when the consultant and consultee are no longer working productively. Termination may be the choice of the consultee or the consultant.

The consultee may believe that the consultation is not being helpful and wish not to continue. There can be many reasons for this belief as discussed in the following sections but the consultant must ultimately accept the decision. At the same time the consultant can politely probe for reasons, and express regret at the decision. The consultant can also offer a referral to others who might be able to help. At the same time the consultant should leave the door open to future consultation, either on the current case, if something changes, or on other issues of concern to the consultee. The school-based consultant will typically still be available and working in the consultee's school.

The consultant may also initiate an early termination of consultation. If the consultant discovers that the relationship between the consultee and client is so negative that the client is in immediate danger of harm, the consultant may need to break confidentiality and take action to prevent further injury. This break, as in other cases of voiding the promise of confidentiality, must be discussed with the consultee.

The consultant initiates termination when no forward progress is being made in consultation. This failure may occur for several reasons, outlined next.

Causes of Consultation Failure

Consultation Failure—Consultant Issues

Consultation failure can certainly fall at the feet of the consultant. Hylander (2004) felt that the chief problem is lack of flexibility on the part of the consultant. Much of the lack of flexibility is in being willing to change the consultant's own conceptualizations (representations) of the problems and to consider a new way of looking at the problem. Another lack of flexibility is failing to shift modes appropriately. That is, consultants must sense when they are challenging too much and return to more nonjudgmental leads and responses and acceptance of the consultee's point of view. The reverse may also be problematic, that is, when the consultant spends too much time accepting the consultee's conceptualization and does not raise different speculations about the causes of the problem and potential solutions. Lack of sensitivity in shifting modes can lead to a number of binds.

Another problem may come from theme interference or countertransference on the part of the consultant. Attitudes developed from previous experiences with others in close relationships of dominance, equality, and subordination, such as parents, teachers, friends, and other persons, may determine the consultant's idiosyncratic, unconscious reactions toward consultees. Such feelings and perceptions, which are not reality based, constitute countertransference attitudes. If acted upon, they can be disruptive to the consultation process (Berlin, 1966). Certain consultee's behavior or appearance may stimulate these attitudes, which in turn leads to failure.

It is obvious that lack of knowledge on the part of the consultant may lead to failure. The consultant need not know much about the consultee's background knowledge in pedagogy, but they should be well trained in psychological theory and in how to apply it in school settings.

The consultant may also lack interpersonal skill. Consultee-centered consultants need to be explicitly educated and supervised in providing consultation. Because skills related to influencing the consultee, maintaining a nonhierarchical relationship, responding to affect, avoiding personal issues, and so on, are difficult to master, practice under controlled conditions is desirable. The consultant is using his or her personality in their work, and other models of providing consultation may be a better fit for the person.

Consultation Failure—Process Issues

The previous chapter reviewed a number of ways the consultation process may head into a blind alley or a bind. Typically this occurs because the consultant is either unable to switch modes as needed or is unable to be flexible in altering his or her representations of the client.

8

Consultation Failure—Consultee Issues

As mentioned in an earlier chapter, consultees need to learn how to be a consultee. They need to accept the nonhierarchical nature of the process and recognize that mutual problem solving requires work on their part. They cannot be passive participants.

Consultation will fail if consultees refuse to take responsibility for their part, however small, in the consultation dilemma. By blaming others, including the client, the consultee may avoid taking action and initiate consultation in search of sympathy and justification for doing nothing.

Consultation will fail if consultees passively and uncritically accept the goals and solutions proposed by the consultant or others. Consultees must engage in the process and feel ownership in any interventions that are produced.

Continued failure with the client prior to consultation can lead to learned helplessness, or the feeling that there is no control over the situation. Learned helplessness can lead to the failure to respond even though there are opportunities to escape from unpleasant circumstances. These feelings can be hard to overcome in consultation and can lead to continued consultee apathy. Consultants can help by pointing out things the consultee can control in interactions with the client.

Disorganized and inconsistent consultees may have difficulty in implementing an intervention effectively. Inconsistency is a major problem in changing behavior. Consultants can point out that new behaviors need to be reinforced continually. Only after clearly establishing the client's new behavior can the teacher shift to a variable schedule of reinforcement.

Other aspects of personality might impact a consultee's preference for consultation style. Consultees with an internal versus external locus of control may be more comfortable with mental health consultation. Consultees who are more authoritarian and dogmatic seem to prefer client-centered rather than consultee-centered consultation (Brown, Pryzwansky, & Schulte, 2011).

Consultation Failure—Client Issues

Some children simply cannot be accommodated in the regular classroom or special education classroom. The consultant and consultee cannot expect to be successful with every client. They must exhaust all feasible efforts to help the child respond to interventions in the consultee's classroom, but referral on to other teams in the school or community for more intensive and specialized help is always an option.

Evaluation Failure

Evaluation is an important part of consultation. If it is not done appropriately consultation efforts may collapse. The consultant and consultee identify client symptoms or problem behaviors in consultation. If a planned, co-constructed intervention is effective, but the evaluation design or measures do not capture data to indicate its success, consultees will reject a valid approach. Technically this is known as a false negative, rejecting a correct hypothesis. Additionally an evaluation can be started or concluded too prematurely, and not detect effects that take time to develop. Consultants should not encourage summative evaluation before the intervention has been implemented with integrity.

Guidelines for Follow-up and Disengagement

Interpersonal-Behavioral

a) Ask debriefing questions to determine success of intervention.
b) Encourage transfer of new learning to other clients.
c) Examine changes in client.
d) Determine the need and willingness to continue to work on this problem and return to the problem identification phase.
e) Examine changes in knowledge, attitude, and objectivity in consultee.
f) Celebrate success.

Intrapersonal-Cerebral

a) Determine whether consultation should continue.
b) Assess whether a conceptual change has occurred.
c) Assess whether the consultee has learned new skills that will be used with future clients.
d) Consider whether an outside referral will be needed for this client.
e) Evaluate reasons for failure if the consultation has not resulted in an improvement in the working relationship between the consultee and client.

Self-Monitoring Questions

a) Should I terminate the consultation now or should I have done it earlier? Did I miss signs that consultation might not work with this client? What could I have done differently?
b) Has my work with this consultee taught me new skills and insights?
c) Could the outcomes have been achieved more easily or more quickly?
d) Am I continuing this consultation to satisfy my own needs?

References

Berlin, I. N. (1966). Transference and countertransference in community psychiatry. *Archives of General of Psychiatry, 15,* 165–175.
Brown, D., Pryzwansky, W. B., & Schulte, A. C. (2011). *Psychological consultation and collaboration.* Upper Saddle River, NJ: Pearson.

Caplan, G. (1970). *The theory and practice of mental health consultation.* New York: Basic Books.

Conoley, J.C., & Conoley, C.W. (1982). *School consultation: A guide to practice and training.* New York: Pergamon Press.

Gagne, R. M. (1985). *The conditions of learning and theory of instruction.* Belmont, CA: Wadsworth.

Gallessich, J. (1982). *The profession and practice of consultation.* San Francisco: Jossey-Bass Publishers.

Garcia, M. (2004). Reflectivity in consultation. In N.M. Lambert, I. Hylander, & J. Sandoval (Eds.), *Consultee-centered consultation: Improving the quality of professional services in schools and community organizations* (pp. 361–374). Mahwah, NJ: Lawrence Erlbaum.

Hylander, I. (2004). Analysis of conceptual change in consultee-centered consultation. In N.M. Lambert, I. Hylander, & J.H. Sandoval (Eds.), *Consultee-centered consultation* (pp. 45–61). Mahwah, NJ: Lawrence Erlbaum.

Mayer, R.E., & Wittrock, M.C. (1996). Problem-solving transfer. In D.C. Berliner & R.C. Calfee (Eds.), *Handbook of educational psychology* (pp. 47–62). New York: Macmillan.

Parsons, R.D., & Meyers, J. (1984). *Developing consultation skills.* San Francisco: Jossey-Bass Publishers.

Perkins, D. N., & Salomon, G. (2012). Knowledge to go: A motivational and dispositional view of transfer. *Educational Psychologist, 47,* 248–258.

Salomon, G., & Perkins, D.N. (1989). Rocky roads to transfer: Rethinking mechanisms of a neglected phenomenon. *Educational Psychologist, 24,* 113–142.

Sandoval, J. (2004). Evaluation issues and strategies in consultee-centered consultation. In N.M. Lambert, I. Hylander, & J. Sandoval (Eds.), *Consultee-centered consultation: Improving the quality of professional services in schools and community organizations* (pp. 393–400). Mahwah, NJ: Lawrence Erlbaum.

11

GROUP CONSULTEE-CENTERED CONSULTATION

The topic of consultation with groups of consultees in the school context has not been written about extensively nor is there a strong research base for practice. Conjoint behavioral consultation does include both parents and teachers in a consultation group and focuses on parents as partners in problem definition and interventions with a child (Sheridan & Kratochwill, 2008). Instructional consultation uses teams of consultants, but the majority of the time one team consultant works with a single teacher consultee (Rosenfield, Silva, & Gravois, 2008). However, it is relatively rare to find accounts of working with multiple teachers or other school personnel as consultees.

Nevertheless, in the consultee-centered consultation and mental health consultation literature there has been some attention to working with groups of consultees. For example, Hylander's work in Sweden is based in part on consultation to the preschool teachers, two or more of whom have responsibility for a group of children. Cohen and Osterweil (1986) report on group mental health consultation with preschool, elementary, and junior high school teachers in Jerusalem. In addition, consultation to groups of new teachers as part of the induction process has also been studied and written about (Babinski & Rogers, 1998; Sandoval, 1977; Wilcox, 1980). Community-based mental health consultants have also worked with teachers and administrators in a group format (e.g., Altrocchi, Spielberger, & Eisdorfer, 1965; Tobiessen & Shai, 1971).

There are a number of institutional-cultural barriers to cooperation among school professionals. The school organization does not often support cooperation between staff members. Teachers work autonomously in their classrooms, with little oversight or supervision. They are relatively independent and have minimal professional contact with other teachers. They are accountable for what happens in their own classroom but not what happens in the school as a whole. When problems arise, typically it falls to them to tackle the problem on their own. Fullan (1996) identifies isolation and lack of collaboration as being two reasons why the teaching profession is "not yet a profession." Principals and other administrators, on the other hand, are responsible for the school as a whole but have minimal influence over what happens to individual children in the classroom. They too are on their own with respect to problem solving. The result is that both teachers and administrators feel powerless to affect change in their own organizational setting (Weinstein, 1979). Group consultee-centered consultation is a vehicle for working together to solve problems in the schools.

Advantages and Disadvantages of Group Consultation

Group consultation has both advantages and disadvantages compared to individual consultation. The choice of working with groups will be determined by practical considerations with respect to the school setting and by consultant training and inclination.

There are several advantages of group consultation. First, working with groups is more efficient than individual consultation in that multiple consultees and clients may be served at one time.

Second, with more participants, more perspectives will be available to examine a problem and generate ideas. There are mutual learning experiences for consultees, which can lead to group cohesiveness in a school. Altrocchi (1972) states, "Peer group influence is often powerful, not only in terms of contributions of others 'in the same boat' and others who have been through the same problems previously, but also in terms of influence on members to see issues in new ways and to try new ways of dealing with problems" (p. 484). There are more points of view available, and it is more likely members will be able to point out cultural stereotypes and common theme problems.

Third, working with groups means that more emotional support is available to the consultee from colleagues. Again, Altrocchi (1972) points out, "Handling of affect by means of encouraging shared expression, opposing transference and regression, supporting defenses such as intellectualization and helping consultees keep some—but not too much—distance from clients can often be accomplished better in group than in individual consultation" (p. 484). Many members may be able to offer realistic reassurance to address shared anxiety. Group members will also be able to support coping strategies as they emerge.

Fourth, because the group has more resources, in the form of group members' experience and training, the consultant will be under less pressure to contribute specific strategies to address the consultee's issues than in individual work. It will be easier to address issues related to lack of knowledge, because there may be information that can be supplied by other peers in the group. In addition, consultees experiencing successful group consultation will feel more comfortable asking for individual consultation for more sensitive issues they are unwilling to bring to group.

There are a number of disadvantages to group consultation as well (Altrocchi et al., 1965). First, organizing a group requires a great deal of time and effort to coordinate the schedules of participants. Teachers have limited free time and teaching obligations during the day. Schedules conflict and overlap. It may be easier to arrange a group for administrators or other personnel who are more flexible, but they too are busy people.

Second, the issue of confidentiality becomes more difficult. In individual consultation, confidentiality is one sided—only the consultant is bound by confidentiality. With multiple consultees, there may be issues individuals do not wish to share with peers because they either do not trust them to keep confidentiality or believe they do not have a "need to know." In group consultation, the participants must recognize and accept that they have obligations to keep information about fellow consultees confidential, particularly from supervisors.

Third, effective group consultation requires the development of a cohesive group willing and interested in the welfare of the participants. Any jealousy, hostility, or conflict among group members will quickly subvert the process. Members who are overly critical of others, judgmental, or domineering can impact the group process.

Fourth, issues springing from theme interference may not be dealt with easily. The consultation methods for dealing with consultee affect may not work, because it is unlikely the members of the group share the exact theme interference, and fellow group members may address the theme too directly (Caplan, 1970). The consultant must particularly guard against the group becoming a psychotherapy group.

Fifth, consultees who lack self-confidence may be too insecure to expose themselves to the group. For these consultees the group can increase anxiety. Others' perceived confidence and skill can elevate certain group members or the consultant to superior status. The insecure consultee will feel out of their league, alone, and demoralized.

There is some evidence, however, that group consultation is more effective than individual consultation when implemented appropriately and the disadvantages ameliorated. Tobiessen and Shai (1971) conducted a program of individual and group consultation in matched sets of schools in four school districts using the same consultants in each condition. Compared to those getting individual consultation, participants receiving group consultation rated the experience more useful and indicated they gained more knowledge regarding child development.

Group consultation may be rare because in many schools, disadvantages may outweigh advantages. Instead of consultation, group work shifts to collaboration as a member of an interdisciplinary team, either in special education individual educational planning, or in student study teams implementing the Response to Intervention framework (Erchul, 2011). Participating as a member of a team offers the school mental health worker an opportunity to use consultation skills, but because of issues such as mandatory participation, and assigned role, it is something different from group consultee-centered consultation.

Preparing for Group Consultation

Assessing Readiness for Group Consultation

Before implementing a program of group consultation, the consultant must conduct a needs assessment to determine if working with groups will be feasible in the setting. In order to complete the needs assessment systematically, the consultant may use a device developed by Davis and Salasin (1975) to examine eight dimensions of organizational readiness (see also Maher & Illback, 1985). By answering questions related to each dimension, the consultant can get an idea of readiness. The system uses the acronym AVICTORY, standing for:

Ability

- Does the consultant have the prerequisite skills and knowledge to do group consultation?
- Are the necessary budgetary, time, and physical resources (space) available?

Values

- Is the consultation program consonant with teacher and administrator professional philosophy and goals?
- Is the consultation program consonant with organizational values as expressed in policies?

Idea

- Is the nature and scope of consultation clear?
- Does the program seem valuable and useful?

Circumstances

- Does the administration support the concept of consultation and will it support a program?

Timing

- Is this the most opportune time to implement a program of consultation?

Obligation

- Is the need for a consultation program apparent to staff and administrators?

Resistance

- Will particular persons or groups significantly resist the program?

Yield

- Are the expected positive outcomes of consultation apparent to staff?

The outcome of the needs assessment (affirmative answers to the previous questions) should help the consultant decide whether to proceed or what additional work needs to be done.

Soliciting Administrative Support for Group Consultation

A program of group consultation, just as with individual consultation, will require a number of systemic changes. In order for the program to be effective, it will be important that it receive explicit administrative support. The administrator will have to support the program with time, space, personnel, coordination, supervision, and training. First, individuals will need to be freed from other duties in order to participate in the program. For example, this means that the demands on school psychologists to test children will need to be reduced in order to free time to talk with teachers. Similarly, a teacher will need to have more released time from classroom instruction in order to participate in consultation. Addressing the time needs for consultation will have to be constantly kept in mind. The temptation will be to use release time provided for consultation for other activities. Administrators will need to protect consultation time.

There will need to be some space provided for the consultation to take place. Although some of these activities may take place in open settings, such as classrooms or the teachers' lounge, there will be a need to provide some small private space to ensure confidentiality. The space should also be free from interruptions so that intensive problem solving can take place.

The administrator can also facilitate group consultation by arranging for professional supervision for the consultant. The consultants will need to review their experiences in consultation with a supervisor and understand where they have been successful and what skills need to be improved.

Finally, there will be a need for continuing education for all the members of the consultation effort. Teachers and other participants will have stopped and thought about what they are doing in the consultation process and will identify needs for new learning and continuing education. Consultants will also need to continue to take workshops, read, and refine their skills.

There will also continue to be a need to meet the mandates of the Individuals with Disabilities Education and Improvement Act. A consultation program is not intended to be a substitution for special education but rather is intended to allow children to receive enhanced services without being removed from the regular classroom or being labeled. One of the driving conceptualizations behind the consultation program is that if it is implemented successfully fewer children will need to be assessed and placed in special education programs. Nevertheless, handicapped children will continue to have a right to services. Because the hope of consultation is to provide help to children as soon as possible, a mechanism, such as the student study team that does not imply special education and provides group consultation, will need to be put in place.

Setting Up a Consultation Group

The first step in implementing group consultation is planning. The consultant will need to make decisions about group size, group composition, location, length of meetings, and duration. The size of the group will depend on both the comfort of the consultant and the existence of naturally occurring groups in the school or district. For example, if there are four third-grade teachers in a school who are interested, that might dictate the size. Generally speaking, groups between five and eight members function well. In larger groups there may be less chance for everyone to participate or have their dilemmas discussed, and in smaller groups it may be more convenient to deal with problems individually because of scheduling issues.

Meeting logistics can also make group work difficult. There will need to be an available room for the meeting at a time members can attend. The room must be private and free from interruptions because of confidentiality issues. Ideally there will be circular seating or other arrangements to facilitate discussion.

Of course there will have to be sufficient time for the meetings. Little can be accomplished in less than 15 minutes with a single consultee and increasing the size of the group increases the amount of time needed so that all can participate. School days are usually divided into periods. The length of the period, for example, 50 minutes, may limit the length of the meeting time. Teachers may be willing to make time for the group before or after the instructional day, and if so, this may simplify time and scheduling issues. Participants may decide to meet each week or on another schedule when all members are available. Consultation meetings may be ongoing or end at the point where participants believe that there has been tangible accomplishment, or there is a natural break in the school year.

The biggest planning issue is group composition. A key to a successful group will be its makeup. A number of factors will need to be taken into account. First is to consider motivation for joining or avoiding a group. Those who initially volunteer to participate in a group may consider themselves to be more professional teachers. The group may gain the reputation of being elitist. Black or other minority teachers may be suspicious and wary of being compared with white teachers, and thus avoid participation.

A second consideration is group homogeneity or heterogeneity. There are well-documented splits in attitude and values between primary and upper grade teachers, between classroom teachers and resource personnel, and between traditionally oriented and progressively oriented teachers (Weinstein, 1979). These splits may cause conflict within the group. Groups that are homogeneous with respect to shared concerns and similar clients may function well. However some mixture of experience, skill, and point of view can make the group more productive. In schools where the ethnicity or culture of the clients is different from the consultee or consultant, having some members sharing the client's ethnicity is very helpful.

A third issue is maintaining group cohesiveness. Trust develops slowly as group members admit mistakes, share vulnerabilities, and offer support without judgment. The consultant must facilitate group cohesion by enforcing rules and reminding participants about confidentiality. Changes in group cohesion may be disrupted if new members are permitted to join an ongoing group.

As mentioned, group consultee-centered consultation has been offered to groups of new and intern teachers (e.g., Babinski, Knotek, & Rogers, 2004). Should they be targeted for group consultation? As novices, they tend to be more anxious about their work, and often have little supervisory support but have high levels of motivation to succeed. Administrators may be reluctant to support group consultation for them, however. Seymour Sarason (1996) commented, "In some instances the principal suggested, and in some cases demanded, that we not go into the classrooms of the new teachers, claiming that the new teacher is very anxious, that she usually has difficulty in matters of discipline, and that she would become more anxious and ineffective if an 'observer' was in the room. Interestingly enough, it was always our experience that in contrast to older teachers the new ones were more likely to seek us out, invite us to their classrooms, and more quickly and openly present their problems" (p. 157). Group consultation is a vehicle for professional development and the creation of a professional identity for this group.

One issue concerns whether the principal or another superior administrator should be allowed to join a group of teachers. Usually this is a bad idea; their participation can stifle group cohesion and openness. Principals have different role demands than teachers, including that of a supervisor, so they are unable to ignore teacher behavior that is ineffective. At the same time, most principals have been teachers and have some expertise that could benefit the group. The principal's role in the school is also that of the leader. This role may cause them to dominate the conversation and implicitly lend more weight to their comments, with the implication that their suggestions should be followed as orders.

On the other hand, if part of a proposed solution to a problem is a change in school-wide policy, having the principal as member may be crucial. Teachers realize in many situations they will be unable take action without principal support. Not having principal involvement on some level, such as a sponsor or promoter if not member, reduces the impact and importance of the group and impedes avenues of change.

Group composition should be directed at increasing the probability of group cohesion. Participation is voluntary and it is difficult to remove someone from a group. However, inviting members who share similar clients with similar demands but have some diversity in background, experience, or training can result in the right mix.

It is usually a good idea to interview each prospective member before the start of the group to clarify the goals of the group and to identify some individual goals of the participants. The consultant can go over the group rules and clarify the consultation contract. Before the first session, all should agree to present their concerns to the group, to engage in mutual problem solving, and to assist and support others solving their work problems.

Selecting a Model

Cohen and Osterweil (1986) discussed two options or models for conducting the group: the case-focused model and the issue-focused model. In the case-focused model, one or two members present a problem they are having with a client. The focus remains on the case with group members exploring the presentation, giving feedback, sharing similar experiences, and offering suggestions for action. The consultant guides the discussion and models professional problem solving. This model is most directly similar to individual consultee-centered case consultation.

The issue-focused model, in contrast, begins when the consultant introduces "a mental health issue or topic that is relevant to a number of cases in different teachers' classrooms and that is generally useful in helping all teachers gain a better understanding of children in their classrooms" (Cohen & Osterweil, 1986, p. 248). The consultant clarifies or defines the issues and is responsible for the pace of the conversation as well as attending to group dynamics. Issues a consultant might introduce include the establishment of classroom routines, discipline problems in the classroom, lack of school motivation, or self-concept in children. The entire group would discuss these issues, and the consultant must be prepared to provide psychological theory and insights into the issues.

Cohen and Osterweil favored the second approach because they claimed it is more likely to engage more of the group members, lead to greater learning, and be more comfortable to insecure consultees. The case-focused model may stimulate defensiveness while presenting a case and amplify feelings of inadequacy. They have data supporting a high level of satisfaction on the part of participants' experience of issue-focused consultation.

The choice of model will be dependent on the consultant's preference and training and on the consultees' experiences. Those who have had successful individual consultee-centered consultation will be comfortable with the first model. Those who have not, or are not comfortable working one-on-one, may prefer the second. Shy or anxious consultees may prefer issue-focused groups. Following a productive experience with issue-focused consultation, consultees may wish to be involved in individual or case-focused consultation.

Group Consultation Stages

In many ways the stages of case-focused group consultee-centered consultation are similar to those of individual consultation. The rapport building, problem identification, intervention, and evaluation are the same with modifications for group participation. Russ (1978) listed four developmental stages: the *relationship development* stage, the *working* stage, the *group autonomy* stage, and *consultee-consultant stage*. The last stage occurs after the group has disbanded.

Relationship Development Stage

The relationship development stage involves attending to issues of entry and reiterating the contract. The first session usually begins with some anxiety and confusion. It is helpful if members know each other, but if not, some ice-breaking exercises are valuable. The consultant introduces the goal of the group, the procedures and rules of the group, and other contractual details. Often the consultant and members of the group will need to withstand a test from other group members. The test consists of introducing an impossible problem to the group to see how the consultant reacts. The consultant must remain calm and nonjudgmental and acknowledge the difficulty of the case but express a willingness to engage with it. The consultant works at developing group cohesion by encouraging all members to participate, enforcing rules such as not interrupting, and acknowledging the legitimacy of different points of view. The consultant reinforces member involvement by reiterating and adhering to the purpose of the group and by connecting concerns that individuals have, saying in effect, "you must have experienced this problem too." The consultant communicates that not all members are expected to agree on an issue. The consultant openly permits and discusses different points of view but represents them accurately and fairly. If there are two points of view, he or she gives credence to both by commenting, "That is another way to look at it." The consultant also shows appreciation for insights with remarks such as, "That is a great point" or "That is interesting" and by encouraging others to do so as well.

The consultant's intent is setting norms for the group. These norms involve encouraging open communication, remaining calm, accepting feelings, and offering nonjudgmental analysis of member contributions. The consultant builds commitment by letting the participants set the agenda and focusing on highly relevant topics.

Working Stage

The working stage begins when the group has grown comfortable with the model of problem solving and the expression of emotion. Babinski et al. (2004) described the process in their new teacher consultation groups: "A teacher presents his or her problem to the group. The facilitators and the group members work together to help the presenting teacher gain a clearer conception of the problem and generate alternative interpretations by asking questions and pushing for clarification and further refinement of the definition of the problem. Once the problem is defined, the group assists the presenting teacher by either discussing additional information needed to understand the problem or brainstorming possible solutions, and developing an initial plan of action. At subsequent meetings the teacher provides follow-up reports on the implementation of the plan, which allows for further exploration and collaborative assistance from the group members" (p. 105).

Steinhauer (2004) identified nine repeating group processes from consultee-centered consultation that contribute to a consultee's perception that the group is instructive and supportive:

(a) Helping members feel understood. Many times teachers believe that only another teacher will truly understand what it is like to teach and manage difficult children. By sharing with other teachers, feelings of isolation, alienation, and excessive responsibility will diminish.

(b) Cognitive reframing. From the cognitive reframing that occurs, the group takes initially overwhelming issues and breaks them down, analyzes them, and puts them in a different perspective. From this process the group member then has a diminished feeling of being out of control and a strategy for addressing the problem.

(c) Teaching. New information that provides fresh ways of understanding or responding to a difficult situation can come from group members or the consultant.

(d) Ventilation. Before cognitive reframing or learning can occur group members need an opportunity for venting in a safe setting the anxious, angry, guilty, discouraged, or depressed feeling generated by a problem. The consultant must recognize when ventilation is sufficient and move the group away from it toward creative problem solving.

(e) Support. Group members in a cohesive group will feel supported when they attempt new techniques and initiatives.

(f) Relief. Participation in a group leads to fewer requests to have the child removed, but when there is such a request, group members come forward to offer respite.

(g) Sense of shared responsibility. Group members feel relief after sharing their dilemma with the group, coming to feel that they do not have to cope with difficult children on their own.

(h) Increased sensitivity to children's needs. With new information and perspective, there is a sense of being able to perceive and respond more effectively to children's needs.

(i) Increased motivation. These processes contribute to increased motivation, a greater sense of accomplishment, and motivation to remain engaged with children despite multiple frustrations.

Autonomy and Consultee-Consultant Stages

The autonomy phase commences when consultees help one another out, and follow the problem solving and conceptual change process on their own with little or no input from the consultant. One part of the group consultation process is for the consultant to reduce the amount of their contributions and to foster self-sufficiency among group members.

A final phase observed by Russ and others is when consultee turns consultant and engages others in discussions outside of the group settings. The participants have internalized the problem-solving techniques used in the group and they apply them in interactions with others.

Consultant Skills

In addition to the skills discussed in previous chapters, involving listening, problem solving, and providing emotional support, the consultant engaging in group consultation needs understanding and skills related to group dynamics and group processes. The consultant functions at least initially as a group leader, and helps organize the group and later manages the group dynamics by setting expectations, encouraging all members to participate, and keeping the group task oriented. The consultant uses the same techniques of one-downsmanship and self-disclosure and models the concerned, nonjudgmental professional approach.

Russ (1978) argues that consultants in group mental health consultation must exhibit the following behaviors aimed at changing the consultee's information processing: (a) didactic teaching; (b) giving direct suggestions and advice; (c) refocusing attention by bringing up or attending to causes, outcomes, and alternatives the consultees have not considered; (d) encouraging the expression of feelings and attitudes; (e) modeling a problem-solving approach that involves scanning information, emphasizing and organizing information, considering different options, and reflecting on personal biases as well as dealing with ambiguity; (f) encouraging consultee information processing; and (g) relinquishing the consultant role to others in the group as appropriate.

Cohen and Osterweil (1986) discussed four roles of the group consultant related to Caplan's taxonomy. To address lack of knowledge, the consultant has an *expert* role in getting group members to share their knowledge from work experience and relating it to theory. "When a specific body of information seems to be lacking, consultants may contribute their expert knowledge by giving a short lecture, or by offering informative remarks at different points of the discussion" (p. 251).

To address lack of skill, the consultant may take a *trainer* role, by arranging group exercises for the group to experiment with and to practice through role playing or other means. "The consultant also trains consultees indirectly by modeling communication and problem-solving skills, which may be internalized and applied by teachers in different situations" (p. 251).

The *affective* role of promoting group cohesion and identification helps promote self-confidence. "[T]he consultant encourages and reinforces the expression of ideas, by listening to participants with respect, by reflecting observed feelings in an accepting manner, by integrating into the discussion useful contributions made by the participants, and by modeling sensitivity to the needs and difficulties of participants, while discouraging judgmental reactions in the group" (p. 251).

The consultant also has a *creative-challenging* role and a *cognitive-reframing* role to combat lack of objectivity. By encouraging group members to share experiences and alternative explanations, consultee themes may be challenged. "The consultant may present provoking examples, challenge accepted 'truisms,' and critically examine evidence for suggested conclusions. The consultant also insists on exploring and analyzing globally described phenomena, so that group members appreciate their complexity and become aware of the possible inter-relations and dynamics of their subsystems and components" (pp. 251–252). Consultants also model personal reflexivity to reevaluate their own behavior and ideas and alternative perspective taking and promote the same behaviors in participants.

Participants

Regular Education Teachers

Regular education teachers will bring to consultation their knowledge of their student (the client), knowledge about the consultation process, and a willingness to talk about the difficulties they are encountering. As the key person in the student's life at school, they are the ultimate consumers of this service. They need to be knowledgeable about the process of consultation to accept its strengths and limitations, and to work at making consultation helpful to themselves.

Resource Teachers

Resource teachers possess a particularly important body of knowledge and expertise that they may offer the regular classroom teacher. They will possess expert knowledge about the special education curriculum, methods, and materials that can be used with children in the classroom, and will be particularly sensitive to the special needs of handicapped children. They will have experienced the frustrations as well as the joys of working with many unusual kinds of children. In their group participation the resource teacher will be able to offer information about instruction as well as provide emotional support for working with challenging children.

School Psychologists

School psychologists bring to the consultation process a knowledge of developmental psychology, learning theory, social psychology, personality dynamics, group dynamics, and family systems. They are able to provide a point of view about how children learn, how their social and emotional development progresses, and how individuals can change. Since they will be drawing on psychological theories as well as their experiences in counseling children, working with the parents, and assessing children's needs, they will offer a perspective quite different from that of the classroom teacher or administrator. As a result of their training they will be skilled in interpersonal relations and should be able to establish productive working relationships with teachers and other members of the special services team and members from other systems, for example, family, probation, hospital, mental health.

School Counselors

School counselors receive training both in emotional development and in interpersonal skills. They will be able to function in many ways like school psychologists in the consultation process. Counselors may also have insight into the interests and vocational needs of children and future educational requirements.

Social Workers

Social workers are particularly knowledgeable about social systems that are interacting to assist children. They are good liaisons to outside institutions such as the courts and the welfare system. They can also play important roles in bridging the home to the school. Knowledge about how these social systems work can assist teachers when their students are involved with multiple systems.

Speech and Language Specialists

Speech and language specialists are knowledgeable about language development and techniques for improving both articulation and language development. When problems center on language difficulties, speech and language specialists may provide a particular insight.

Administrators

Administrators may also be the recipients of group consultation and should profit from examining their day-to-day activities and difficulties. It will often be fruitful to employ consultative efforts to look at the entire system of the school. Districts will need to know whether resources are being provided to teachers in appropriate ways and whether there is support for the utilization of these services. Group consultation can help with this problem solving.

Guidelines for Group Consultation

Interpersonal–Behavioral

a) Obtain administrative sanction and support for group consultation.
b) Solve logistical problems.
c) Select and interview prospective participants to create a productive group.
d) Choose the issue-focused or case-focused model.
e) Establish ground rules and norms for the group members.

Intrapersonal–Cerebral

a) Determine if group consultation is feasible in this setting.
b) Determine institutional readiness for group consultation.
c) Evaluate if the group is being productive.

Self-Monitoring Questions

a) Do I have the group-process skills to be successful in group consultation?
b) Am I willing to give up control of the process to the group at some point?
c) Would some of the consultees be better served in individual consultation?
d) Are the participants supporting each other as planned or should I address some destructive practices appearing in the group?
e) Do I have the right mix of participants?
f) Have I been able to use the same productive practices in the group that I have in individual consultation?
g) Am I helping the group address individual consultees' difficulties around lack of knowledge, skill, confidence, and objectivity?

References

Altrocchi, J. (1972). Mental health consultation. In S.E. Golann & C. Eisdorfer (Eds.), *Handbook of community mental health*. New York: Appleton-Century-Crofts.

Altrocchi, J., Spielberger, D.D., & Eisdorfer, C. (1965). Mental health consultation with groups. *Community Mental Health Journal, 1,* 127–134.

Babinski, L.M., Knotek, S.E., & Rogers, D.L. (2004). Facilitating conceptual change in new teacher consultation groups. In N.M. Lambert, I. Hylander, & J.H. Sandoval (Eds.), *Consultee-centered consultation* (pp. 101–113). Mahwah, NJ: Lawrence Erlbaum.

Babinski, L.M., & Rogers, D.L. (1998). Supporting new teachers through consultee-centered group consultation. *Journal of Educational and Psychological Consultation, 9,* 285–308.

Caplan, G. (1970). *The theory and practice of mental health consultation*. New York: Basic Books.

Cohen, E., & Osterweil, Z. (1986). An "issue-focused" model for mental health consultation with groups of teachers. *Journal of School Psychology, 24,* 243–256.

Davis, H.T., & Salasin, S.E. (1975). The utilization of evaluation. In E.L. Struening & M. Guttentag (Eds.), *Handbook of evaluation research* (Vol. 1). Beverly Hills, CA: Sage.

Erchul, W.P. (2011). School consultation and response to intervention. *Journal of Educational & Psychological Consultation, 21,* 191–208.

Fullan, M. (1996). Professional culture and educational change. *School Psychology Review,* *25,* 496–500.

Maher, C.A., & Illback, R.J. (1985). Implementing school psychological service programs: Description and application of the DURABLE approach. *Journal of School Psychology,* *23,* 81–89.

Rosenfield, S.A., Silva, A., & Gravois, T.A. (2008). Bringing instructional consultation to scale. In W.P. Erchul & S.M. Sheridan (Eds.), *Handbook of research in school consultation* (pp. 203–223). New York: Erlbaum/ Taylor & Francis.

Russ, S.W. (1978). Group consultation: Key variables that effect change. *Professional Psychology,* *9,* 145–152.

Sandoval, J. (1977). Mental health consultation for teachers in preservice training. *California Journal of Teacher Education, 3,* 110–124.

Sarason, S.B. (1996). *Revisiting "The culture of the school and the problem of change."* New York: Teachers College Press.

Sheridan, S.M., & Kratochwill, T.R. (2008). *Conjoint behavioral consultation* (2nd ed.). New York: Springer.

Steinhauer, P.D. (2004). Thirty years of consulting to child welfare. In N. M. Lambert, I. Hylander, & J. H. Sandoval (Eds.), *Consultee-centered consultation* (pp. 149–170). Mahwah, NJ: Lawrence Erlbaum.

Tobiessen, J., & Shai, A. (1971). A comparison of individual and group mental health consultation with teachers. *Community Mental Health Journal, 7,* 218–226.

Weinstein, R.S. (1979, September). Group consultation in school settings: Constraints against collaboration. Paper presented at the annual meeting of the American Psychological Association, New York.

Wilcox, M.R. (1980). Variables affecting group mental health consultation for teachers. *Professional Psychology, 11,* 728–732.

12
ETHICAL ISSUES IN CONSULTEE-CENTERED CONSULTATION

Rather than abstract, universal prescriptions to follow in the execution of professional practice, ethical principles have come about as a result of many years of empirical experience by thoughtful professionals. They function to remind consultants of the common pitfalls our predecessors have experienced. Most ethical issues and dilemmas serve as danger signals advising the consultant to proceed forward with great caution, and possibly to change to another path. This chapter will not review the whole of professional ethics, as useful as that might be. Instead the reader can review professional codes of ethics such as those of the American Psychological Association (APA, 2002, 2010). Rather the focus will be on how to cope with the ambiguous and ever-present problem of ethics in consultative relationships within schools.

There are two primary areas that present difficulties for consultants. The first concerns what the consultant brings to the consultative relationship. They bring an ethical and philosophical paradigm and its relationship to the change process, and they bring their level of self-awareness and insight into their own motivations.

The second area consists of some ethical issues likely to occur at some point during consultation. These issues relate to consultee rights, client rights, parental rights, and organizational rights.

Consultant Issues Ethical and Philosophical Positions

Consultee-centered consultants, accepting the constructivist origins of our practice, recognize that neither consultant nor their professional relationships are value-free and objective. Consequently, we are forced to confront ourselves with questions about what our values are, how they might be different than those with whom we work, and how we must respond to the differences, especially during this time of expanded diversity in our schools.

"The consultant must clarify for himself his own particular goals and motivations for influencing others" (Lippitt, 1959, p. 7). In the schools the question becomes why are we working with teachers and other educational personnel to "help" them enhance or increase their skills in working with children? Of course, "enhance what skills?" is an ethical question in itself in the sense of who chooses the skills and what those skills might be. First let us focus on the consultant's need to clarify his or her own philosophical model of the change process. The model should explicate the goals of the process and the process by which they are to be achieved.

It is helpful to examine a classic confrontation of values in the helping professions (Davis & Sandoval, 1982). The confrontation was between Carl Rogers and B.F. Skinner (1956) over the issues involved in the control of human behavior. Skinner's argument was that it is inevitable that forces (e.g., political) will attempt to control human behavior, so shouldn't we base the control on intelligent planning and positive reinforcement rather than on the lack of planning and negative reinforcement exemplified by our legal justice system? Rogers's position was that one could avoid the ethical issue of control of human behavior by choosing the proper goals and techniques in human relationships.

Kelman (1990), commenting on these positions, pointed out that Rogers fails to recognize that he is engaged in the control of the client's behavior. On the other hand Skinner is intoxicated with the goodness of what he is doing for and to the client, which in turn leads to a failure to recognize the ambiguity of the control that he exercises. Kelman argued that the manipulation of the behavior of others is always an ethically ambiguous act, even when the manipulation is aimed at positive behavioral change (Kelman, 1990). There is a two-horned dilemma confronting the consultant: Any manipulation of human behavior inherently violates a fundamental value of human freedom, but there is no formula for structuring an effective change situation such that manipulation is totally absent. It is well established that consultation is an interpersonal influence process (Erchul, Grissom, & Getty, 2008; Meyers, Parsons, & Martin, 1979) and the consultant must face this dilemma. In order to promote the enhancement of freedom of choice as a positive goal in spite being in a position of influence, the consultant must be aware of conditions favoring a consultee's ability to exercise choice and to maximize his or her individual values and provide them.

Erchul (2009) argued that Caplan accepted that consultee-centered consultants are attempting to influence the consultee in order to foster problem ownership and sustained commitment to action. The consultant's behavior during the initial phases of consultation, building relations and maintaining rapport, have the result of establishing the soft power base of the consultant. This power base allows the consultee the most protection against manipulation. The consultant is serving as a model, establishes expertise in psychology, and offers information. By volunteering for consultation and understanding the terms of the consultee-centered consultation contract, the consultee has a right to expect that the consultant will act to help the "consultee overcome his weaknesses and remedy his shortcomings" (Caplan & Caplan, 1993, p. 352).

The problem of manipulation is made even more difficult and complicated in consultee-centered consultation, in that the consultant hopes not only to influence the consultee to change and become more effective, but also to influence the behavior of the consultee's client to change, a third party with whom the consultant has minimal contact and who the consultant may never have direct dealings!

There is no easy way out of this struggle and every professional must come to his or her own terms with the situation. Nevertheless, the consultee-centered consultant must wrestle particularly with two key issues. The first issue is whether he or she has a sufficient understanding of the institution and its structure, the values of the community, the variety of cultures within the community, and differences in culture between consultee and client, consultant and consultee, and consultant and client. This knowledge helps us to ensure that we are not merely imposing our values (Runquist & Behar, 1974). The second issue is whether he or she is helping to create situations that promote reflection, introspection, and the opportunity to make choices (Kelman, 1990). To use Benne's (1961) terminology, the consultant must ask, "Am I using democratic ethics in dealing with my consultees and their clients?"

Benne's Democratic Ethical Principles

Benne's explication of democratic ethics can help school-based consultation to cope with the vagaries and ambiguities inherent in ethical dilemmas. What follows is a paraphrase with citations from Benne's (1961) chapter on guiding principles for consultants.

Principle 1: The consultative process must be collaborative (see also Lambert, 1974). This means that the consultant needs to approach the situation with an understanding that he or she does not have the "answer," but that through consultation an approach or intervention can emerge with which both consultant and consultee can feel comfortable. Consultants need to maintain their sense of ethical integrity by not supervising the consultee, but they also must not compromise themselves into agreeing to an intervention proposed by the consultee if it violates the consultants' ethical standards.

Principle 2: Consultation must be educational for the consultee. In other words, the consultant "must leave the persons with whom he works better equipped to solve the particular problem which he has helped them to solve [and] . . . better equipped to solve subsequent problems" (Benne, 1961, p. 144).

Principle 3: Ideas and interventions emerging from the consultative process must be considered experimental. Ideas must be considered hypotheses to be tested and possibly modified as a result of a fair trial. "Planned arrangements must be seen by those who make them as arrangements to be tested in use and to be modified in terms of their human effects when tried" (Benne, 1961, p. 144).

Principle 4: The consultation must be task-oriented and client-centered. Any changes or new intervention the consultee is to make is only for the purpose of working more effectively with the client, not to change the consultee for "his or her own good." Nor should the interventions be "oriented to the maintenance or extension of the prestige or power of those who originate contributions" (Benne, 1961, p. 145). Here again, an experimental rather than dogmatic stance is required regardless of the status of those involved in the consultative process.

Principle 5: Consultation should provide interventions that are "anti-individualistic, yet provide for the establishment of appropriate areas of privacy and for the development of persons as creative units of influence in our society" (Benne, 1961, p. 146). That is, any intervention needs to recognize that any one individual is not entitled to encroach on the rights of others, yet neither can a person's individuality be hampered or totally subjected to the good of the classroom. This balance of considerations can be particularly difficult when the consultation is focused on a child exhibiting a behavioral problem.

These principles are not the answers, only guidelines for consultee-centered consultation. The consultant will still have to engage in critical thinking and appraisal.

Consultant Self-Awareness

It should be obvious that a consultant's own personality, both the strengths and weaknesses, can enhance or interfere with the consultative relationship. Consultation is no different in this regard than counseling, psychotherapy, or any other interpersonal interaction. Does this mean that in order to be an effective consultant we need to be in perfect mental health or free from idiosyncratic biases? Clearly this is impossible. What it does mean is that the consultant needs to recognize that self-awareness is important and to keep working towards the goal of self-knowledge all the while knowing that it is a goal never to be achieved.

Issues may arise in the consultant's life that temporarily affect their emotional state. In addition issues from relationships from the past may reemerge to reduce the consultant's objectivity. This matter is addressed in the APA *Ethical Principles of Psychologists and Code of Conduct* in section 2.06 on Personal Problems and Conflicts: "(a) Psychologists refrain from initiating an activity when they know or should know that there is a substantial likelihood that their personal problems will prevent them from performing their work-related activities in a competent manner. (b) When psychologists become aware of personal problems that may interfere with their performing work-related duties adequately, they take appropriate measures, such as obtaining professional consultation or assistance and determine whether they should limit, suspend or terminate their work-related duties" (APA, 2002, p. 5).

In the consultation literature this situation is most often conceptualized as countertransference difficulties (Berlin, 1966; Caplan, 1970). Berlin (1966) defined countertransference as "remnants from old relationships which determine the [consultant's] idiosyncratic, unconscious reactions toward his co-workers, supervisors, subordinates, and the people he and they serve" (p. 166). If these remnants remain out of the awareness of the consultant they manifest themselves in ways that can prove destructive to the consultative relationship.

How can the consultant become more aware of these kinds of issues and render them less likely to interfere in the consultant's professional work? Berlin (1966) has suggested that having received personal therapy is helpful. Supervision both during training and at stressful times in later life is essential to competent functioning. If formal supervision is not available, peer evaluation and review are two other excellent ways of getting feedback on work performance. Otherwise the consultant is left with taking time and reflecting on what has happened in a consultation session, and evaluating the thoughts and feelings that have been stimulated by the case. The effective practitioner constantly considers how they could improve.

Professional isolation is dangerous. Two situations having to do with job demands isolate school consultants. The first relates to physical separation. Frequently, the working situation in schools is such that consultants rarely come into contact with their professional colleagues or supervisors. They are often the only mental health expert assigned to a school. All their professional time is spent with consultees and clients. This fact is unfortunate because working with people is too complex a process for consultants not to be able to have ongoing help and support.

The second form of isolation is self-isolation or complacency. Complacency occurs when the consultant feels that he or she knows all there is to know and begins to stagnate. There are many reasons for this type of behavior but professional burnout is certainly one (Maslach, Schaufeli, & Leiter, 2001). Often very difficult cases are brought to consultation and good intentioned work does not have a dramatic payoff. The consultant, feeling hopeless, begins to dehumanize consultees and clients.

Another factor in complacency is the absence of an evaluation protocol to provide feedback on changes in consultee and client behavior. Too often consultees enjoy the time they spend with the consultant but do not enact changes in their classroom or school. The consultant must guard against self-isolation and take steps to ameliorate the situation before they, as consultants, become part of the problem.

There are times when the consultant becomes aware of system dynamics that really cannot be addressed by a consultant perceived to be within the system. In these instances it is probably best to involve an outside consultant to help clarify and differentiate systems that form individual issues and to identify the relationships.

Knowing One's Limits

Consultants are often placed in situations where their consultees expect them to perform miracles. The consultee may be so lacking in knowledge, skill, and objectivity, that they will be unable to change their behavior or alter their relationship with the client. Or, the client may be so disabled, disturbed, and out of control that almost nothing can be done for them in the current school situation.

When consultants begin to get out of their areas of comfort or expertise they should refer the consultee (or client) to a professional within whose realm of expertise that service falls. If no such person exists, or is already overburdened, or the consultee or client refuses to avail him or herself of the referred professional's expertise, the consultant's conscience, after professional soul-searching, must be the final arbiter.

Specific Ethical Dilemmas

There are several specific issues that school-based consultee-centered consultants often face. These issues can be considered from the point of view of the rights of consultees, clients, parents, and the educational system (Hughes, 1986). Issues include confidentiality, privacy, client welfare, and informed consent.

Consultee Rights

Confidentiality

Two primary issues for school-based consultants surface under this heading. They are concerns about consultee confidentiality and concerns about client confidentiality. Client confidentiality will be covered in the next section.

Most writers (e.g., Boehm, 1956; Caplan, 1970; Hughes, 1986) have expressed the need for consultants to maintain confidentiality in the consulting relationship. All that is said between consultant and consultee should be kept confidential by the consultant. Otherwise the trust that is essential for the relationship to begin and to be maintained will never be formed, and the consultee will continue to censor thoughts. However, confidentiality is one-sided and is held by the consultee. The consultee is free to discuss any or all of what has transpired but the consultant is not.

This situation becomes an ethical issue when other teachers, administrators, or parents try to get information from the consultant about a teacher or other school personnel with whom the consultant is working. The consultant might be approached directly or in a more cloaked or gossipy fashion. It is not unusual for administrators who have not accepted the consultation contract to insist that school-based consultants inform on or evaluate a teacher. It is obvious that if the consultant acquiesces, the relationship with that particular teacher and with most teachers that hear of the incident will deteriorate. Guidance from APA (2010) is for the consultant to clarify the reason for confidentiality, explain their commitment to professional ethics, and take reasonable steps to resolve the conflict ethically.

Privacy

Consultee-centered consultation is directed at solving work-related problems. The consultant must be careful not to ask questions or solicit information about the consultee's private life. When personal issues come up, the consultant must gently turn the conversation back to a focus on the client. Hughes (1986) provided an example: "when a teacher-consultee states that her recent divorce has left her low on energy, the consultant empathizes, saying 'We professionals have personal lives, too, that sometimes demand a great deal from us.' Then, the consultant refocuses the discussion on the consultation problem" (p. 493).

Goal Conflicts

The consultant may have different goals for the consultation and for the client. The consultant may wish to help the child succeed in the classroom and restore the relationship between the teacher and child, whereas the consultee may wish to have the child removed and placed in special education. The consultant must not gloss over such conflicts but acknowledge them and attempt to reach a compromise, if possible. For example, in the previous scenario, the consultant might say, "The child may indeed need special educational assistance, but it will take weeks or months for that to be arranged, and can we think together now about what we might do in the meantime?" If the consultant and consultee cannot reach a compromise, the consultant must end the consultation.

Informed Consent

Consultees need to know what they are getting into. This is usually handled by the consultant's introduction during the initiation phase. Consultees must be informed that consultation is voluntary, that they will still maintain primary responsibility of the client, that they are free to reject suggestions from the consultant, and that the consultation process will take time and has no guarantees of success.

Client Rights

Confidentiality

Sharing information about a client of the consultee is an issue that has received less attention in terms of confidentiality. School-based consultants will often have information from a confidential file, from other professionals who have worked with the client, from testing and interviews with the client, or from the client's parents that the consultee or community-based consultant would not have. What or how much of this information should be shared with other professionals or paraprofessionals with whom the consultant is working regarding the client?

Again, there is no hard and fast rule. On the one hand, the consultant never shares specific information received in a situation where confidentiality has been assured either explicitly or implicitly. On the other hand, generalizations, never specifics, from confidential situations might be shared with others with whom the consultant is working if those generalizations are essential to the understanding and resolution of the client's difficulty. The consultant should be sure that those with whom he or she works understand the concept of confidentiality and the consultant should stress that such shared information be kept confidential. The principle of sharing information on a "needs-to-know" basis seems sensible.

Client Welfare

In traditional consultee-centered consultation (Caplan, 1970) the consultee is the person who has primary responsibility for the client. Caplan stated, "in consultee-centered consultation, improvement in [the] client is a side effect, welcome though it may be, and the primary goal is to improve the consultee's capacity to function effectively in this category of case, in order to benefit many similar clients in the future" (Caplan, 1970, p. 125).

In the schools, however, the consultant also owes an obligation to see to the client's welfare. However, the consultant usually can only exercise indirectly this responsibility through the work of other adults. As a result, the consultants fulfill their responsibility to the client by providing support and insights via consultation.

How this becomes an ethical problem is that to advocate for a child in a potentially harmful situation it is usually the case that the contract made with the consultee must be broken. Two parts of the formal or informal consulting contract are that the consultant is a consultant and not a supervisor (e.g., is not here to evaluate the consultee's job performance) and that the consultant maintains confidentiality (e.g., not repeat the content of consultation discussions). Therefore, in order to advocate for a child one of these two "rules" must almost always be broken. Either the consultant decides that the consultee is in a position to do the client harm and must be stopped (breaking the rule that the consultant is nonjudgmental and not evaluative) or, the consultee has revealed something during a conversation that causes the consultant concern for the client's welfare (the consultant must break confidentiality).

When client welfare is threatened, breaking the consulting contract may be the ethical thing to do. The APA (2002) Ethical Principles state: "(b) Psychologists disclose confidential information without the consent of the individual only as mandated by law, or where permitted by law for a valid purpose such as to (1) provide needed professional services; (2) obtain appropriate professional consultations; (3) protect the client/patient, psychologist, or others from harm" (Principle 4.05 (b) p. 7).

Clearly then, this is done only when there is danger to the client and, unless in a crisis situation, after the consultant has exhausted all his or her professional expertise, gotten outside help in trying to deal with the situation and exhausted any other avenues of intervention. The consultant must inform the consultee that he or she cannot maintain silence and of the reason behind the decision to disclose information to others. This is not to be an "easy-out" for a difficult consultation, only a last resort.

The two situations that most often arise, which may call for this type of intervention, are when a teacher, administrator, or support service personnel is experiencing a psychiatric crisis, or when one of these persons is experiencing such severe theme interference (Caplan, 1970) that harmful effects are likely to befall the client.

Parent Rights

Parental Permission

The school-based consultant will have to respect the due process and equal protection rights of parents. Either the consultant or consultee will need to inform parents to receive their permission for their children to be seen as part of consultative activities (if the consultant and consultee decide direct contact with the child would be appropriate and useful to problem solving). At some point consultees must at least inform parents of concerns about their children and might involve them in the course of gathering data about the client. In addition the teacher consultees might seek help in consultation from the consultant about how to speak with parents in preparing for a parent contact. As appropriate, even if there is no referral for special education, parents should participate in the consultation process and should be brought into the educational planning when needed. A sample set of guidelines on parent involvement might include:

1. Contact parents whenever someone other than his or her teacher will be interviewing the child.
2. Contact parents whenever an intervention in the classroom is outside of customary educational practice.
3. Contact parents whenever a child will be individually assessed by anyone.
4. Contact parents whenever information from the home will be useful in problem solving.
5. Contact parents whenever an intervention in the classroom may be supported by an intervention at home.

In general, when the intervention is centered on the consultee and not the child, and the changes are within the scope of normal teacher behavior, the parents need not be informed. If they can help, or if their child is being treated differently from other children, parents should give informed consent. Parents should be approached with care and may become part of the consultation process as consultees.

School Rights
Contractual Clarity

Contractual clarity can be most difficult to maintain in a school setting. Chapter 3 includes some guidelines for establishing a consultation contract with administrators. Problems can develop after the consultant has obtained sanction to proceed, however. This is particularly true in a small school district where someone in a role such as a school psychologist, counselor, or social worker could be asked to assume a variety of responsibilities, for example, a psychologist who is also director of the special education program. The additional role of supervisor could easily place the psychologist in the awkward position of having to supervise the same special education teacher with whom he or she wishes to serve as consultant. These sorts of dual relations are not uncommon and need to be recognized and avoided.

The district is not the only source of pressures. Teachers and other school personnel can also place conflicting demands on the consultee-centered consultant. Upon discovering oneself in a conflicting situation, the consultants should state their consultation role as clearly as possible and as often as necessary and not waver from that role with their consultees (Gallessich, 1974). In particular, the mental health consultant is often, either overtly or covertly, requested to do psychotherapy with his or her consultee. The consultant is ethically bound not to lapse into psychotherapy with the consultee even if both the consultant and consultee feel psychotherapy is called for. The consultant cannot allow him or herself to be coerced, seduced, or manipulated into any role inappropriate to the negotiated contract.

Another common situation found in schools is a tendency toward gossiping and rumor spreading. The consultant cannot resort to or allow him or herself to be manipulated into gossiping about the client, the consultee, or others concerned with the client. This can be especially difficult if the social pressures are such that to be accepted into the school this type of behavior is "required." Obviously the consultant cannot engage in this kind of behavior, even when pressured; hopefully, the consultant's behavior will be a model for others.

Evaluation

Another of the consultant's roles maybe that of a program evaluator, particularly in small districts where responsibilities vary. Consultants in this position should process data only and not be placed in the position of making any personal evaluations or judgments about anyone with whom he or she is also consulting.

The consultant also has an ethical responsibility to the district to evaluate the outcomes of their services. The evaluation may be a report on the aggregate results of individual consultation evaluations, or a more comprehensive look at the impact of consultation on consultees and on the school as a system.

Values versus Techniques

"Value considerations present themselves intertwined with cognitive and technical considerations, and it is often difficult to sort out the value component of decisions and judgments from other components when it needs to be most confronted in its own right" (Bennis, Benne, & Chin, 1969, p. 580). Consultants must try to monitor professional behavior well enough to ensure that they do not attempt to impose their own personal paradigm on others with whom they work by couching values in technical terms and psychological jargon. Nor can consultants allow themselves to become lulled into thinking that any action they take during a professional interaction is ipso facto a matter of technique free from values. Professionals need not be inhibited and overcautious, but should take a good hard look at themselves. Values are intertwined with professional performance. It should not be otherwise. Without our values we would be less than human. But let us not indulge in delusions of being beyond values or of being able to suspend them at a moment's notice. Rather, let us be aware of them and incorporate them into our total character as adult persons.

Obviously this brief chapter is only an exposure to some of the ethical demands that will be placed upon school-based consultants. Consultee-centered consultants need not become philosophers of ethics, but should become aware of the role that ethics, values, and self-awareness play in their professional life and act in a responsible manner to make good ethical decisions.

References

American Psychological Association. (2002). Ethical principles of psychologists and code of conduct. *American Psychologist, 57,* 1060–1073.

American Psychological Association. (2010). 2010 amendments to the 2002 "Ethical principles of psychologists and code of conduct." *American Psychologist, 65,* 493.

Benne, K.D. (1961). Democratic ethics and human engineering. In K.D. Benne, W. Bennis, & R. Chin (Eds.), *The planning of change* (pp. 141–148). New York: Holt, Rinehart & Winston.

Bennis, W. G., Benne, K. D., & Chin, R. (1969). Some value dilemmas of the change agent. In W. G. Bennis, K. D. Benne, & R. Chin (Eds.), *The planning of change* (2nd ed.) New York: Holt, Rinehart & Winston.

Berlin, I.N. (1966). Transference and countertransference in community psychiatry. *Archives of General Psychiatry, 15,* 165–172.

Boehm, W. (1956). The professional relationship between consultant and consultee. *American Journal of Orthopsychiatry, 26,* 241–248.

Caplan, G. (1970). *The theory and practice of mental health consultation.* New York: Basic Books.

Caplan, G., & Caplan, R. B. (1993). *Mental health consultation and collaboration.* San Francisco: Jossey-Bass.

Davis, J.M., & Sandoval, J. (1982). Applied ethics for school-based consultants. *Professional Psychology, 13,* 543–551.

Erchul, W.P. (2009). Gerald Caplan: A tribute to the originator of mental health consultation. *Journal of Educational and Psychological Consultation, 19,* 95–105.

Erchul, W.P., Grissom, P.F., & Getty, K.C. (2008). Studying interpersonal influence within school consultation. In W.P. Erchul & S.M. Sheridan (Eds.), *Handbook of research in school consultation* (pp. 293–322). New York: Erlbaum/ Taylor & Francis.

Gallessich, J. (1974). Training the school psychologist for consultation. *Journal of School Psychology, 12,* 138–149.

Hughes, J.N. (1986). Ethical issues in school consultation. *School Psychology Review, 15,* 489–499.

Kelman, H.C. (1990). Manipulation of human behavior: An ethical dilemma for the social scientist. *Prevention in Human Services, 8,* 23–41.

Lambert, N.M. (1974). A school-based consultation model. *Professional Psychology, 5,* 267–275.

Lippitt, R. (1959). Dimensions of the consultant's job. *Journal of Social Issues, 15,* 5–12.

Maslach, C., Schaufeli, W.G., & Leiter, M.P. (2001). Job burnout. *Annual Review of Psychology, 52,* 397–422.

Meyers, J., Parsons, R.D., & Martin, R. (1979). *Mental health consultation in the schools.* San Francisco: Jossey-Bass.

Rogers, C.R., & Skinner, B.F. (1956). Some issues concerning the control of human behavior. *Science, 124,* 1057–1066.

Runquist, M.P., & Behar, L.B. (1974, April). Prevention of mental health problems: Meeting needs or imposing values. Paper presented at the convention of the American Orthopsychiatric Association, San Francisco, CA.

INDEX

program evaluation 164; Rogers and
Skinner confrontation and 156; school
rights 164; values vs. techniques 165
*Ethical Principles of Psychologists and Code
of Conduct* (American Psychological
Association) 155, 160, 162; Personal
Problems and Conflicts 158
evaluating outcomes: changes in client
behavior 128–9; changes in consultee
attitude and affect 130–1; changes in
consultee behavior 129–30; evaluating
the consultant 131; evaluation theory
and 127; questions for 127–8; *see also*
follow-up and disengagement stage
(step 8)
evaluations: ethical responsibility and 164;
failure of 135–6; formative 116–17,
118; local 32; *see also* follow-up and
disengagement stage (step 8)
evaluation theory 127; *see also* follow-up
and disengagement stage (step 8)
evidence-based theories, for interventions
102–6
Executive Function concept 65, 67
expectations 36–9, 60–1, 93
experimental attitude: components of
113–14; fostering with "I don't know"
100
experimental mind-set 55
experimental nature, of human services
consultation 3, 38
experimental process 56, 157
experiments: defined 113; *see also*
information sharing, hypothesis
generation, and reframing stage
(step 4); supporting interventions and
experimentation stage (step 7)
expert consultation 1
expert role 149
eye contact 40

failure: of consultations/interventions 113,
117, 126, 133–6; *see also* blind alleys;
follow-up and disengagement stage
(step 8)
false turning 119
family background 68
family-school cooperation, for
interventions 109
feedback 131
flexibility, lack of and failure 134
follow-up and disengagement stage
(step 8) 27, 125–37; background 125;

changes in client behavior (evaluating)
128–9; changes in consultee attitude
and affect (evaluating) 130–1; changes in
consultee behavior (evaluating) 129–30;
consultant evaluation 131; consultation
failure—client issues 135; consultation
failure—consultant issues 134;
consultation failure—consultee issues
135; consultation failure—process issues
134; evaluation failure 135–6; guidelines
for 136; step 1: debriefing 125–7, 126t;
step 2: facilitating transfer 127; step 3:
evaluating outcomes 127–31; step 4:
disengagement and termination process
132–3; timing of disengagement 132–3;
see also blind alleys
formative evaluations 116–17, 118
frame of reference 104
free association mode, boredom during
(Hylander) 120
freedom of choice 156
free neutral mode (Hylander) 18, 54
Freudian theory 6, 103
fundamental attribution errors 52

Gagne, Robert 86, 105
generating interventions stage (step 6)
27, 97–111; Adult Behavior
Change Theory 107; after problem
identification, data collection, and
forming a working hypothesis 98;
asking "what do other teachers do
with this problem?" 99; asking "what
has worked for other children in
analogous circumstances?" 99; asking
"what have you already done to address
this problem?" 99; background and
review 97–8; child-focused vs. system-
focused 108; cognitive psychology and
104–5; conceptualization and 98–9;
consultant saying "I don't know"
99–100; criteria for choosing among
interventions (Davis and Sandoval)
108–9; culturally relevant interventions
106–7, 107t; developmental theory
and 102–3; ecological theory and 108;
generalizations across theories 105–6;
guidelines for 109–10; intervening with
the consultee 106; intervention defined
97; intervention planning conversation
107–9; prescriptive intervention 100–102;
psychodynamic theory and 103–4;
social learning theory and 104; social

psychology and 105; theory-based/
evidence-based interventions 102–6
goal conflicts 161
gossip 34, 160, 164
grade levels, children's preparedness/
readiness for 86–7
grilling questions 49
Grimes, Jess, *Psychological Approaches to
Problems of Children and Adolescents* 101
grounded theory 18
group consultee-centered consultation
133, 139–53; administrators in 145, 151;
advantages of 140; AVICTORY (ability,
values, idea, circumstances, timing,
obligation, resistance, yield, Davis &
Salasin), for assessing readiness 142–3;
background 139–40; behaviors aimed
at changing the consultee's information
processing (Russ) 149; case-focused
model for 146; cohesiveness of groups
145; composition of groups 144–6;
consultants skills 149–50; disadvantages
of 139–40, 141; guidelines for 152;
homogeneity/heterogeneity of groups
144–5; Individuals with Disabilities
Education and Improvement Act and
143; institutional-cultural barriers to
cooperation 139–40; issue-focused
model for 146; nine repeating group
processes (Steinhauer) 148; regular
education teachers in 150; resource
teachers in 150; school counselors in
151; school psychologists in 150–1;
setting up/planning for 144–6; social
workers in 151; soliciting administrative
support for 143–4; speech and language
specialists in 151; stage 1: relationship
building stage 147; stage 2: working
stage 147–8; stage 3: autonomy stage
149; stage 4: consultee-consultant
stage 149
guidelines for consultants 27–8; analyzing
and considering the context for
intervention 93–4; data gathering
(additional) 68; ethical issues/dilemmas
157–8; follow-up and disengagement
136; generating interventions 109–10;
group consultations 152; information
sharing and hypothesis generation 79;
joint guidelines with administrators
32; orientation: building relationships
and maintaining rapport 44–5; problem
exploration/definition/reframing 57;

supporting interventions and
experimentation 122
Guvà, Gunilla, questions to assist
consultees 51, 52*t*

halo effect 76
Harris, A.H. 44
health and development information 64
helping professions, consultation in the
1–3
Henning-Stout, M., three views of
constructivism 15–16
hidden fight, the (Hylander) 120
hierarchical learning (Gagne) 86, 104–5
high-road vs. low-road transfer 127
home environments, of children and
performance in school 84–5
homework, mutual 62
Hughes, J.N. 32, 38, 161
human freedom 156
human services consultation 2–3; *see also*
mental health consultation
humor 117
Hylander, I. 134, 139; blind alleys in the
consultation process 118–22; magic
turning 97, 132; modes of interaction
18–19, 54; terms 39–40, 47–8, 78; *see
also* blind alleys
hypotheses: attribution errors and 52;
creating a new working hypothesis
78; experiments and 113, 157;
generation of and reframing 77–8, 98;
see also information sharing, hypothesis
generation, and reframing stage (step 4)

identification, simple 25
"I don't know" response 99–100
indirect questions 49
indirect services 3
individual differences domains: Cognitive
Capacity 65, 66*f*, 67; Engagement
Capacity 66*f*, 67; Personal Dispositions
66*f*, 67; Social Capacity 66*f*, 67
Individuals with Disabilities Education and
Improvement Act 143
inference questions 49
inferences, for interventions 78
information sharing/hypothesis
generation/reframing stage (step 4) 27,
71–9; avoiding the authority position 72;
cognitive biases 75–6; confirmatory and
disconfirmatory information 74; creating
a new hypothesis 78; drawing inferences

nice party, the (Hylander) 119
Noell, G.H., treatment integrity 115–18
noise, in the classroom 84
non-consultant roles 60
nonhierarchical relationships 98, 134
non-human services consultation 1–2
nonverbal nuances: during disengagement
133; electronic data sharing and 77;
intervention support and 117–18;
responses to feelings 40–1
normative data 73
novice consultants: complexity of problems
and 47; interventions and 97–8, 101
nursery schools 22

objectivity, lack of 5, 20t, 24–5, 53, 60, 150,
160
observation, for data gathering 63, 78
Oka, E.R. 107t
one-downsmanship 42, 43, 72, 100
opened-ended questions 49
open stance 40
organization development theory and
technique 82; see also analyzing systemic
forces stage: context for intervention
(step 5)
orientation stage: relationship building and
maintaining rapport (step 1) 27, 31–46;
active listening 39–40; confidentiality
and 37–8, 41; consultee silence (using
and responding to) 42; contracts and
37–8; cultural issues 42–3; duration of
consultation 37; establishing proximity
33–5; expectations and 36–8; four
concerns of consultants (Kelly) 36;
guidelines for 32, 44–5; initiating
consultation 35; negotiating a role with
administrators 31–3; nonverbal response
to feelings 40–1; one-downsmanship
and 42; preparing teachers and other
consumers 38–9; reluctance and
resistance and 44; responding to
compliments 42; responding to questions
from the consultee 41; verbal response to
feelings 41; willingness checks 44
Osterweil, Z. 139, 146, 149–50
outcomes, unanticipated 115
over-involvement 61

pace, of information sharing 73
paperwork, excess for teachers and
administrators 87, 90
parameters of consultation 3–4, 4t

paraphrasing 39
parental permission 163
parent conferencing skills 85
parent rights 163
parents, home environments and school
support and 84–5
Parker, B. 5; list of common teacher beliefs
22–3
passivity 135
peer relationships 98, 130; group
consultation and 140; see also group
consultee-centered consultation
peer review 131, 159
permissiveness 22
Personal Dispositions domain 66f, 67
personal involvement, direct 25–6
Personal Problems and Conflicts
(American Psychological Association)
*Ethical Principles of Psychologists and Code
of Conduct* 158
philosophical positions: for consultants
155–7; see also ethical issues/dilemmas
Piaget, Jean, "American Question, The"
103
pioneers, in the field of mental health
consultation 5–7
planning, for consultation groups 144–6
planning conversation, for interventions
107–9
play therapy 103
portfolios, data gathering and 64
power struggles 78
*Prescriptions for Children with Learning and
Adjustment Problems* (Blanco) 100–1
prescriptive interventions 100–2
presentation 47–8
prevention and consultee-centered
consultation 8–11, 109; levels of
(primary, secondary, tertiary) 9–10
preventive psychiatry movement 5
primary prevention 9–10
priority setting 56–7
privacy, of consultees 161
Problem Analysis Interview (PAI) 50
problem exploration/definition/reframing
stage (step 2) 3, 27, 47–58, 63, 98, 125;
accessible reasoning 54–5; attribution/
bias errors 52; cognitive behavioral model
and 50–1; conceptual change 55; cultural
issues and 53; dangers in using questions
49–50; dimensions of the problem
56–7; direct and indirect questions 49;
focus on the client 50–1; focus on the

Made in the USA
San Bernardino, CA
24 August 2018